Come Follow

A lively and interesting collection of
poems for young children which has already
delighted thousands of readers
all over the world

Come Follow Me

BELL & HYMAN

Published in 1983 by
Bell & Hyman Limited
Denmark House
37–39 Queen Elizabeth Street
London SE1 2QB

First paperback edition 1966
Fifteenth printing 1985
Originally printed in 1956 by
Evans Brothers Limited
© Bell & Hyman Limited 1983

ISBN 0 7135 2359 X

Set in 9 on 11pt Baskerville
and printed in Great Britain by
Cox & Wyman Ltd, Reading

Contents

Nursery Rhymes
and Traditional Verse,
Poems for the Young

PART ONE

Round about in a fair ring-a,
Thus we dance and thus we sing-a

Bell horses, bell horses,
What time of day?
One o'clock, two o'clock,
Three and away.

Round about in a fair ring-a,
Thus we dance and thus we sing-a;
Trip and go, to and fro,
Over this green-a;
All about, in and out,
Over this green-a.

A cat came fiddling out of a barn,
With a pair of bagpipes under her arm,
She could sing nothing but 'Fiddle-de-dee.
The mouse has married the bumble bee.'
Pipe, cat – dance, mouse —
We'll have a wedding at our good house.

If all the seas were one sea,
What a great sea that would be!
If all the trees were one tree,
What a great tree that would be!
And if all the axes were one axe,
What a great axe that would be!
And if all the men were one man,
What a great man that would be!
And if the great man took the great axe
And cut down the great tree,
And let it fall into the great sea,
What a splish-splash that would be!

Once I saw a little bird going hop, hop, hop.
So I cried, 'Little bird, will you stop, stop, stop?'
And was going to the window to say 'How do you do?'
When he shook his little tail and away he flew.

8

'Little girl, little girl
  Where have you been?'
'Gathering roses
  To give to the Queen.'
'Little girl, little girl,
  What gave she you?'
'She gave me a diamond
  As big as my shoe.'

Girls and boys come out to play,
The moon doth shine as bright as day;
Leave your supper and leave your sleep,
And come with your playfellows in the street,
Come with a whoop and come with a call,
Come with a goodwill or not at all.
Up the ladder and down the wall,
A halfpenny roll will serve us all.
You find milk and I'll find flour,
And we'll make a pudding in half an hour.

  Where are you going,
  My little kittens?

  We are going to town
  To get us some mittens.

  What! mittens for kittens!
  Do kittens wear mittens?
  Who ever saw little kittens with mittens?

  Juniper, Juniper,
    Green in the snow;
  Sweetly you smell
    And prickly you grow.

  Juniper, Juniper,
    Blue in the fall:
  Give me some berries,
    Prickles and all.

The first of April, some do say,
Is set apart for All Fools' Day,
But why the people call it so
Nor I nor they themselves do know.

The dove says, Coo,
What shall I do?
I can hardly maintain my two.
Pooh, says the wren,
Why, I've got ten
And keep them all like gentlemen!

Little Boy Blue, come, blow up your horn,
The sheep's in the meadow, the cow's in the corn;
But where is the boy that looks after the sheep?
He is under the haystack, fast asleep.
Will you wake him? No, not I;
For if I do, he'll be sure to cry.

Said a frog on a log,
'Listen, little Bunny.
Will you ride by my side?
Wouldn't that be funny!'

Peter and Michael were two little menikin,
They kept a cock and a fat little henikin;
Instead of an egg, it laid a gold penikin,
Oh, how they wish it would do it againikin!

Rock-a-bye, baby, thy cradle is green;
Father's a nobleman, mother's a queen;
And Betty's a lady, and wears a gold ring;
And Johnny's a drummer, and drums for the king.

Where are you going,
My little cat?

I am going to town,
To get me a hat.

What! a hat for a cat!
A cat get a hat!
Who ever saw a cat with a hat?

A man went a-hunting at Reigate;
He wished to jump over a high gate.
    Said the owner, 'Go round,
    With your gun and your hound,
For you never shall jump over my gate.'

Pussy Cat, Pussy Cat, where have you been?
I've been to London to look at the Queen.

Pussy Cat, Pussy Cat, what did you there?
I frightened a little mouse under the chair.

Ride a-cock horse to Banbury Cross,
To see a fine lady upon a white horse;
Rings on her fingers and bells on her toes,
She shall have music wherever she goes.

There was a little dog, and he had a little tail,
    And he used to wag, wag, wag it.
But whenever he was sad because he had been bad,
    On the ground he would drag, drag, drag it.

He had a little nose, as of course you would suppose,
    And on it was a muz-muz-muzzle,
And to get it off he'd try till a tear stood in his eye,
    But he found it a puz-puz-puzzle.

A farmer went trotting on his grey mare,
    Bumpety, bumpety, bump!
With his daughter behind him so rosy and fair,
    Lumpety, lumpety, lump!

A raven cried 'Crook' and they all tumbled down,
    Bumpety, bumpety, bump!
The mare broke her knees, and the farmer his crown,
    Lumpety, lumpety, lump!

The mischievous raven flew laughing away,
    Bumpety, bumpety, bump!
And said he would serve them the same the next day,
    Lumpety, lumpety, lump!

Whether the weather be fine, or whether the weather be not,
Whether the weather be cold, or whether the weather be hot,
We'll weather the weather, whatever the weather,
    Whether we like it or not.

THREE RIDDLES

The man in the wilderness asked of me
How many strawberries grew in the sea.
I answered him, as I thought good,
As many red herrings as grew in the wood.

In Spring I look gay
Deck'd in comely array,
In Summer more clothing I wear;
When colder it grows
I fling off my clothes,
And in Winter quite naked appear.
                    (*Answer :* A Tree.)

I have a little sister, they call her Peep, Peep,
She wades the water so deep, deep, deep;
She climbs the mountains, high, high, high;
Poor little creature, she has but one eye.
                    (*Answer :* A Star.)

LITTLE DAME CRUMP

Little Dame Crump, with her little hair broom,
One morning was sweeping her little bedroom,
When, casting her little grey eyes on the ground,
In a sly little corner a penny she found.

'Ods bobs!' cried the Dame, while she stared with surprise.
'How lucky I am! bless my heart, what a prize!
To market I'll go, and a pig I will buy,
And little John Gubbins shall make him a stye.'

So she washed her face clean, and put on her gown,
And locked up the house, and set off for the town;
When to market she went, and a purchase she made
Of a little white pig, and a penny she paid.

When she'd purchased the pig, she was puzzled to know
How they both should get home, if the pig would not go;
So fearing lest piggie should play her a trick,
She drove him along with a little crab stick.

Piggie ran till they came to the foot of a hill,
Where a little bridge stood o'er the stream of a mill;
Piggie grunted and squeaked, but no farther would go;
Oh, fie! Piggie, fie! to serve little Dame so.

She went to the mill, and she borrowed a sack
To put the pig in, and took him on her back;
Piggie squeaked to get out, but the little Dame said,
'If you won't go by fair means, why, you must be made.'

At last to the end of her journey she came,
And was mightily glad when she got the pig hame;
She carried him straight to his nice little stye,
And gave him some hay and clean straw nice and dry.

With a handful of peas then Piggie she fed,
And put on her night-cap and got into bed;
Having first said her prayers, she extinguished the light
And being quite tired, we'll wish her good night.

One, two,
　　Buckle my shoe;
Three, four,
　　Knock at the door;
Five, six,
　　Pick up sticks;
Seven, eight,
　　Lay them straight;
Nine, ten,
　　A good fat hen.
Eleven, twelve,
　　Dig and delve;
Thirteen, fourteen,
　　Maids a-courting;
Fifteen, sixteen,
　　Maids in the kitchen;
Seventeen, eighteen,
　　Maids a-waiting;
Nineteen, twenty,
　　My plate's empty.

AN OLD RHYME

I went to market and bought me a Cat.
Cat had four legs, I had but two.
'Tis almost midnight, what shall I do?

I went a little further and found me a Dog.
Dog wouldn't carry the cat; Cat wouldn't goo.
'Tis almost midnight; what shall I do?

I went a little further and found me a Boy.
Boy wouldn't carry the dog;
Dog wouldn't carry the cat; Cat wouldn't goo.
'Tis almost midnight; what shall I do?

I went a little further and found me a Stick.
Stick wouldn't beat the boy;
Boy wouldn't carry the dog
Dog wouldn't carry the cat; Cat wouldn't goo.
'Tis almost midnight; what shall I do?

I went a little further and found me a Fire.
Fire wouldn't burn the stick;
Stick wouldn't beat the boy;
Boy wouldn't carry the dog;
(Repeat as before.)

I went a little further and found me some Water.
Water wouldn't quench the fire;
Fire wouldn't burn the stick;
(Repeat as before.)

I went a little further and found me an Ox.
Ox wouldn't drink the water;
Water wouldn't quench the fire;
(Repeat as before.)

I went a little further and found me a Butcher.
Butcher wouldn't kill the ox;
Ox wouldn't drink the water;
(Repeat as before.)

I went a little further and found me a Rope.
Rope wouldn't hang the butcher;
(Repeat as before.)

I went a little further and found me some Grease.
Grease wouldn't grease the rope;
(Repeat as before.)

I went a little further and found me a Rat.
Rat began to eat the grease; Grease began to grease the rope;
Rope began to hang the butcher; Butcher began to kill the ox;
Ox began to drink the water; Water began to quench the fire;
Fire began to burn the stick; Stick began to beat the boy;
Boy began to carry the dog; Dog began to carry the cat;
Cat began to goo,
So now it's all over and I am happy.

When the wind is in the east,
'Tis good for neither man nor beast;
When the wind is in the north,
The skilful fisher goes not forth;
When the wind is in the south,
It blows the bait in the fishes' mouth
When the wind is in the west,
Then 'tis at the very best.

THE HOUSE THAT JACK BUILT

This is the house that Jack built.

This is the malt
That lay in the house that Jack built.

This is the rat
That ate the malt
That lay in the house that Jack built.

This is the cat
That killed the rat
That ate the malt
That lay in the house that Jack built.

This is the dog
That worried the cat
That killed the rat
That ate the malt
That lay in the house that Jack built.

This is the cow with the crumpled horn
That tossed the dog
That worried the cat
That killed the rat
That ate the malt
That lay in the house that Jack built.

This is the maiden all forlorn
That milked the cow with the crumpled horn
That tossed the dog
That worried the cat
That killed the rat
That ate the malt
That lay in the house that Jack built

This is the man all tattered and torn
That kissed the maiden all forlorn
That milked the cow with the crumpled horn
That tossed the dog
That worried the cat
That killed the rat
That ate the malt
That lay in the house that Jack built.

This is the priest all shaven and shorn
That married the man all tattered and torn
That kissed the maiden all forlorn
That milked the cow with the crumpled horn
That tossed the dog
That worried the cat
That killed the rat
That ate the malt
That lay in the house that Jack built

This is the cock that crowed in the morn
That waked the priest all shaven and shorn
That married the man all tattered and torn
That kissed the maiden all forlorn
That milked the cow with the crumpled horn
That tossed the dog
That worried the cat
That killed the rat
That ate the malt
That lay in the house that Jack built.

SIMPLE SIMON

Simple Simon met a pieman
  Going to the fair;
Said Simple Simon to the pieman,
  'Let me taste your ware.'

Says the pieman unto Simon,
  'Show me first your penny';
Says Simple Simon to the pieman,
  'Indeed I have not any.'

Simple Simon went a-fishing
  For to catch a whale;
All the water he had got
  Was in his mother's pail.

Simple Simon went to look
  If plums grew on a thistle;
He pricked his fingers very much
  Which made poor Simon whistle.

A RHYME FOR WASHING HANDS

Wash, hands, wash,
  Daddy's gone to plough.
Splash, hands, splash,
  They're all washed now.

THE QUEEN BEE

When I was in the garden,
  I saw a great Queen Bee;
She was the very largest one
  That I did ever see.
She wore a shiny helmet
  And a lovely velvet gown,
But I was rather sad, because
  She didn't wear a crown.

Mary K. Robinson

THE MOUSE, THE FROG AND THE LITTLE RED HEN

Once a Mouse, a Frog, and a Little Red Hen,
   Together kept a house;
The Frog was the laziest of frogs,
   And lazier still was the Mouse.

The work all fell on the Little Red Hen,
   Who had to get the wood,
And build the fires, and scrub, and cook,
   And sometimes hunt the food.

One day, as she went scratching round,
   She found a bag of rye;
Said she, 'Now who will make some bread?'
   Said the lazy Mouse, 'Not I.'

'Nor I,' croaked the Frog as he drowsed in the shade,
   Red Hen made no reply,
But flew around with bowl and spoon,
   And mixed and stirred the rye.

'Who'll make the fire to bake the bread?'
   Said the Mouse again, 'Not I,'
And, scarcely op'ning his sleepy eyes,
   Frog made the same reply.

The Little Red Hen said never a word,
   But a roaring fire she made;
And while the bread was baking brown,
   'Who'll set the table?' she said.

'Not I,' said the sleepy Frog with a yawn;
   'Nor I,' said the Mouse again.
So the table she set and the bread put on,
   'Who'll eat this bread?' said the Hen.

'I will!' cried the Frog. 'And I!' squeaked the Mouse,
   As they near the table drew;
'Oh, no, you won't!' said the Little Red Hen,
   And away with the loaf she flew.

A PARTY SONG

Merry have we met
And merry have we been;
Merry let us part,
And merry meet again

With a merry sing-song,
Happy, gay and free,
With a merry ding-dong
Again we'll happy be.

THE PANCAKE

Mix a pancake,
Stir a pancake,
Pop it in the pan.

Fry the pancake,
Toss the pancake,
Catch it if you can.

Christina Rossetti

RAIN

Pitter, patter, hear it raining?
Slow at first, then faster, faster.
Put on your raincoat,
Hold up your umbrella,
Pull on your Wellingtons
And splash in the puddles.

1. *Children clap hands slowly and lightly, gradually getting faster and louder.*

2. *They pretend to button up raincoats, open umbrellas and pull on Wellington boots.*

3. *They stamp their feet on the ground.*

Lilian McCrea

THE DONKEY

My donkey has a bridle
    Hung with silver bells,
He feeds upon the thistles
    Growing on the fells.
The bells keep chiming, chiming
    A little silver song;
If ever I should lose him
    It would not be for long.

Rose Fyleman

BOOTS AND SHOES

My Wellington boots go
Thump-thump, thump-thump,
My leather shoes go
Pit-pat, pit-pat,
But my rubber sandals
Make no noise at all

1. *Children beat loudly on the floor with their feet.*
2. *They beat softly with their feet.*
3. *They beat with their feet making no noise at all.*

Lilian McCrea

THE DANDELION PUFF

The dandelion puff
    Is a very queer clock,
It doesn't say tick,
    And it doesn't say tock,
It hasn't a cuckoo,
    It hasn't a chime,
And I really don't think
    It can tell me the time!

Mary K. Robinson

SEVEN LITTLE PIGS

Seven little pigs went to market,
  One of them fell down;
One of them, he ran away,
  And five got to town.

FINGER FOLK
(*Putting on gloves*)

Finger Folk, Finger Folk,
Four Fairy Finger Folk;
Wearing suits of leather,
All of them together —
  Funny Finger Folk!

Finger Folk and Thumb-man,
Short, sturdy Thumb-man:
Just as quaintly dressed
In a leather vest —
  Funny Thumb-man!

H. M. Tharp

GETTING UP

When I get up in the morning
I'll tell you what I do,
I wash my hands and I wash my face,
Splishity-splash, splishity-splash.
I clean my teeth till they're shining white,
Scrubbity-scrub, scrubbity-scrub,
Then I put on my clothes and brush my hair,
And runnity-run, I run downstairs.

Children dramatize all the actions as they say the story. For the last line they raise both arms and lower them quickly, making running movements with their fingers.

Lilian McCrea

I SPY

One, round the candytuft,
  Two, round the tree,
Three, round the hollyhock,
  Then find me.

Candytuft! Hollyhock!
  Where can you be?
I've looked in front, I'll look behind,
  One – two – THREE!

N. E. Hussey

THE DISAPPOINTED SHRIMPER

My net
Is heavy with weed.
My net
Is heavy indeed
With wet,
Wet weed.

For an hour I tried,
For two, for three,
I fished,
I kept looking inside
My net to see
Some shrimps for tea.
I wished
For shrimps for tea.

And the day is done,
And I haven't one
Shrimp
          for
                    tea.

P. A. Ropes

KIND DEEDS

Little drops of water,
  Little grains of sand,
Make the mighty ocean,
  And the pleasant land.

Thus the little minutes,
  Humble though they be,
Make the mighty ages
  Of eternity.

Little deeds of kindness,
  Little words of love,
Make this earth an Eden
  Like the heaven above.

Isaac Watts

HIDE AND SEEK

Baby loves to play with me,
  Peek-a-boo! Peek-a-boo!
She goes and hides behind a tree,
  I see you! I see you!

Baby is so very wee,
Hiding's easy as can be!

Phyllis Drayson

MY TOYS

My red engine goes chuff-chuff-choo! chuff-chuff-choo!
My shiny drum goes rum-tum-tum, rum-tum-tum.
My teddy bear goes gr . . . grrr . . . grrr . . .
And my wooden bricks go clitter-clatter, clitter-clatter, rattle-
    bang – BUMP!

Lilian McCrea

HERE WE COME A-HAYING

Here we come a-haying,
  A-haying, a-haying,
Here we come a-haying,
  Among the leaves so green.

Up and down the mower goes
  All the long field over,
Cutting down the long green grass,
  And the purple clover.

Toss the hay and turn it,
  Laid in rows so neatly,
Summer sun a-shining down,
  Makes it smell so sweetly.

Rake it into tidy piles
  Now the farmer's ready,
Load it on the old hay cart,
  Drawn by faithful Neddy.

Down the lane the last load goes,
  Hear the swallows calling.
Now at last our work is done,
  Night is softly falling.

Eunice Close

THE DRAGON

What do you think? Last night I saw
  A fiery dragon pass!
He blazed with light from head to tail,
  As though his sides were glass.

But when my Mummie came to look
  Out through the window-pane,
She laughed, and said: 'You silly boy —
  It's an electric train!'

Mary Mullineaux

THE BELLS OF LONDON

Gay go up and gay go down,
To ring the bells of London town.
    Halfpence and farthings,
        Say the bells of St Martin's.
            Oranges and lemons,
                Say the bells of St Clement's.
    Pancakes and fritters,
        Say the bells of St Peter's.
            Two sticks and an apple,
                Say the bells of Whitechapel.

Kettles and pans,
Say the bells of St Ann's.
    You owe me ten shillings,
        Say the bells of St Helen's.
            When will you pay me?
                Say the bells of Old Bailey.
    When I grow rich,
        Say the bells of Shoreditch.
Pray when will that be?
Say the bells of Stepney.
    I am sure I don't know,
        Says the great bell of Bow.

THE DUSTMAN

Every Thursday morning
Before we're quite awake,
Without the slightest warning
The house begins to shake
        With a Biff! Bang!
        Biff! Bang! Biff!
It's the Dustman, who begins
        (BANG! CRASH!)
To empty all the bins
Of their rubbish and their ash
        With a Biff! Bang!
        Biff! Bang! Bash!

Clive Sansom

A GIANT'S CAKE

Each year I have a birthday,
  When people buy me toys,
And mother gives a party
  To lots of girls and boys.

I have a cake with candles,
  And icing, pink and white,
With rosy candles lighted,
  It makes a lovely sight.

Each year the cake grows larger,
  Another light to take,
So if I grow much older
  I'll need a giant's cake.

Evelina San Garde

WASH-DAY

This is the way we wash our clothes,
  Rub-a-dub-dub, rub-a-dub-dub!
Watch them getting clean and white,
  Rub-a-dub-dub, rub-a-dub-dub!

This is the way we mangle them,
  Rumble-de-dee, rumble-de-dee!
Round and round the handle goes,
  Rumble-de-dee, rumble-de-dee!

This is the way we hang them out,
  Flippity-flap, flippity-flap!
See them blowing in the wind,
  Flippity-flap, flippity-flap!

This is the way we iron them
  Smooth as smooth can be!
Soon our wash-day will be done,
  Then we'll all have tea.

Lilian McCrea

CONVERSATION

Mousie, mousie,
Where is your little wee housie?
  Here is the door,
  Under the floor,
    Said mousie, mousie.

Mousie, mousie,
May I come into your housie?
  You can't get in,
  You have to be thin,
    Said mousie, mousie.

Mousie, mousie,
Won't you come out of your housie?
  I'm sorry to say
  I'm busy all day,
    Said mousie, mousie.

Rose Fyleman

THE BALLOON MAN

This is a little 'action poem' for the littlest ones, in which five children
may take part. It includes some useful 'colour training'.

Characters :   *Properties :*
Balloon man   Coloured balloons
Mother
Three children

Balloon Man :
I stand here every afternoon,
Waiting for someone to buy a balloon.
Look at the colours bright and gay.
Just one penny is all you pay.
Plenty for all who come, have I,
Come and buy! Come and buy!

First Child:
    I have a penny, Mother said,
    So I think I'd like one of red.

Second Child:
    I would like that one of green.
    It is the prettiest that I've seen.

Third Child:
    Lucky am I, please give me two,
    One of yellow, and one of blue.

Balloon Man:
    Now with your balloons just run and play,
    I like to see you happy and gay.
    (*Children play with balloons.*)

Mother:
    Children! Children! Come home to tea!

First Child:
    That is my Mother calling me.

All Together:
    Balloon man, don't go away,
    We'll come and see you another day.
    (*Children run out saying* 'Good-bye!')

                                        E. Herbert

TO THE BAT

    Little bat, little bat,
        Pray, when you speak,
    Speak a bit louder,
        You've such a high squeak,
    That only those people
        With quite a good ear,
    Who know all about you,
        Can possibly hear.

                                        Edith King

FEET

Big feet,
Black feet,
Going up and down the street;
Dull and shiny
Father's feet,
Walk by me!

Nice feet,
Brown feet,
Going up and down the street;
Pretty, dainty,
Ladies' feet,
Trip by me!

Small feet,
Light feet,
Going up and down the street;
Little children's
Happy feet,
Run by me!

Suggestions for rhythmic actions:
Children are arranged in three groups:
1. *Tall children or boys, slow walking step;*
2. *Girls, quick walking or tripping;*
3. *Smallest children, running.*
Each Group interprets movements of verses as indicated by words. The verses
are spoken by one child or in Choric Speech by several children.

Irene Thompson

TO LET

Two little beaks went tap! tap! tap!
Two little shells went crack! crack! crack!
Two fluffy chicks peeped out, and oh,
They liked the look of the big world so,
That they left their houses without a fret
And two little shells are now TO LET.

D. Newey-Johnson

CALENDAR RHYME

January falls the snow,
February cold winds blow,
In March peep out the early flowers,
And April comes with sunny showers.
In May the roses bloom so gay,
In June the farmer mows his hay,
In July brightly shines the sun,
In August harvest is begun.
September turns the green leaves brown,
October winds then shake them down,
November fills with bleak and smear,
December comes and ends the year.

Flora Willis Watson

HIGH JUNE

Fiddle-de-dee!
Grasshoppers three,
Rollicking over the meadow;
Scarcely the grass,
Bends as they pass,
So fairy-light is their tread, O!

Said Grasshopper One,
'The summer's begun,
This sunshine is driving me crazy!'
Said Grasshopper Two,
'I feel just like you!'
And leapt to the top of a daisy.

'Please wait for me!'
Cried Grasshopper Three,
'My legs are ready for hopping!'
So grasshoppers three,
Fiddle-de-dee,
Raced all the day without stopping.

C.A. Morin

MY NEW UMBRELLA

I have a new umbrella,
A bright red new umbrella,
A new red silk umbrella,
   I wish that it would rain,

And then I could go walking,
Just like a lady walking,
A grown-up lady walking
   Away 'way down the lane.

I could not step in puddles,
The shiny tempting puddles,
No lady walks in puddles,
   Then turn, and home again.

M. M. Hutchinson

HONEY BEAR

There was a big bear
Who lived in a cave;
His greatest love
Was honey.
He had twopence a week
Which he never could save,
So he never had
Any money.
I bought him a money-box
Red and round,
In which to put
His money.
He saved and saved
Till he got a pound,
Then spent it all
On honey.

Elizabeth Lang

THE BUS

There is a painted bus
  With twenty painted seats.
It carries painted people
  Along the painted streets.
They pull the painted bell,
  The painted driver stops,
And they all get out together
  At the little painted shops.

'Peter'

DANCING ON THE SHORE

(Ten in circle. Queen in centre.)

Ten little children
  Dancing on the shore;
The queen waved a royal wand
  And out went four.

(Four step outside circle.)

Six little children
  Dancing merrily;
The queen waved a royal wand
  And out went three.

(Three step out and join hands with four, making an outside circle around the smaller one.)

Three little children
  Danced as children do;
The queen waved a royal wand
  And out went two.

(Two join larger circle.)

One little maiden,
  Dancing just for fun;
The queen waved a royal wand
  And out went one.

M. M. Hutchinson

FISH AND BIRD

How happy to be a fish,
To dive and skim,
To dart and float and swim
And play.

How happy to be a bird,
To fly and sing,
To glide on feathered wing
All day.

Rosemary Brinckman

THE SNOWMAN

Come in the garden
  And play in the snow,
A snowman we'll make,
  See how quickly he'll grow!
Give him hat, stick, and pipe,
  And make him look gay,
Such a fine game
  For a cold winter day!

E. M. Adams

THINGS I LIKE

I like blowing bubbles, and swinging on a swing;
I love to take a country walk and hear the birdies sing.

I like little kittens, and I love puppies too;
And calves and little squealing pigs and baby ducks, don't you?

I like picking daisies, I love my Teddy bear;
I like to look at picture books in Daddy's big armchair.

Marjorie H. Greenfield

THE POSTMAN

Rat-a-tat-tat, Rat-a-tat-tat,
 Rat-a-tat-tat tattoo!
That's the way the Postman goes,
 Rat-a-tat-tat tattoo!
Every morning at half-past eight
You hear a bang at the garden gate,
And Rat-a-tat-tat, Rat-a-tat-tat,
 Rat-a-tat-tat tattoo!

Clive Sansom

MY NEW RABBIT

We brought him home, I was so pleased,
 We made a rabbit-hutch,
I give him oats, I talk to him,
 I love him very much.

Now when I talk to Rover dog,
 He answers me 'Bow-wow!'
And when I speak to Pussy-cat,
 She purrs and says 'Mee-ow!'

But Bunny never says a word,
 Just twinkles with his nose,
And what that rabbit thinks about,
 Why! no one ever knows.

My Mother says the fairies must
 Have put on him a spell,
They told him all their secrets, then
 They whispered, 'Pray don't tell.'

So Bunny sits there looking wise,
 And twinkling with his nose,
And never, never, never tells
 A single thing he knows.

Elizabeth Gould

35

A WATERING RHYME

Early in the morning,
  Or the evening hour,
Are the times to water
  Every kind of flower.
Watering at noonday,
  When the sun is high,
Doesn't help the flowers,
  Only makes them die.

Also, when you water,
  Water at the roots;
Flowers keep their mouths where
  We should wear our boots.
Soak the earth around them,
  Then through all the heat
The flowers will have water
  For their thirsty 'feet'!

P. A. Ropes

PUSSY-CAT AND PUPPY-DOG

Mee-ow, mee-ow,
Here's a little pussy-cat
With furry, furry fur,
Stroke her very gently
And she'll purr, purr, purr.

Bow-wow, bow-wow,
Here's a little puppy-dog
With a wiggly-waggly tail,
Pat him and he'll wag it
With a wiggy-wag-wag
And a waggy-wag-wag.

Lilian McCrea

I SAW A SHIP A-SAILING

I saw a ship a-sailing,
  A-sailing on the sea;
And, oh! it was laden
  With pretty things for me.

There were comfits in the cabin,
  And apples in the hold;
The sails were made of silk,
  And the masts were made of gold.

The four-and-twenty sailors
  That stood between the decks,
Were four-and-twenty white mice,
  With chains about their necks.

The Captain was a duck,
  With a packet on his back,
And when the ship began to move,
  The Captain said, 'Quack, quack!'

IF

If I take an acorn
  That's fallen from its cup,
And plant it in the garden
  And never dig it up;
The sun and rain will change it
  To a great big tree,
With lots of acorns on it
  Growing all for me.

I'll plant an orange pippin,
  And see what that will do;
I hope an orange tree will grow,
  I think it will, don't you?
If oranges should really grow,
  And if there should be many,
I'll put them in a basket
  And sell them two a penny.

Alice Todd

JOHNNY'S FARM

Johnny had a little dove;
   Coo, coo, coo.
Johnny had a little mill;
   Clack, clack, clack.
Johnny had a little cow;
   Moo, moo, moo.
Johnny had a little duck;
   Quack, quack, quack.
Coo, coo; clack, clack; moo, moo; quack, quack;
Down on Johnny's little farm.

Johnny had a little hen;
   Cluck, cluck, cluck.
Johnny had a little crow;
   Caw, caw, caw.
Johnny had a little pig;
   Chook, chook, chook.
Johnny had a little donkey;
   Haw, haw, haw.
Coo, coo; clack, clack; moo, moo; quack, quack;
Cluck, cluck; caw, caw; chook, chook; haw, haw;
Down on Johnny's little farm.

Johnny had a little dog,
   Bow, wow, wow;
Johnny had a little lamb,
   Baa, baa, baa;
Johnny had a little son,
   Now, now, now!
Johnny had a little wife,
   Ha! ha!! ha!!!
Coo, coo; clack, clack; moo, moo; quack, quack;
Cluck, cluck; caw, caw; chook, chook; haw, haw;
Bow-wow; baa, baa; now, now; ha! ha!!
Down on Johnny's little farm.

H. M. Adams

JUST LIKE THIS

Action Rhyme

The trees are waving to and fro,
  Just like this; just like this;
Branches swaying high and low,
  Just like this; just like this.

The waves are tossing up and down,
  Just like this; just like this;
On the sand lies seaweed brown,
  Just like this; just like this.

The birds are always on the wing,
  Just like this; just like this;
Bees are humming in the ling,
  Just like this; just like this.

The gnats are darting through the air,
  Just like this; just like this;
Dragon-flies flit here and there,
  Just like this; just like this.

Squirrels are racing up the trees,
  Just like this; just like this;
Rabbits scurry o'er the leas,
  Just like this; just like this.

Forest ponies frisk and prance,
  Just like this; just like this;
Little children play and dance,
  Just like this; just like this.

D. A. Olney

HOW MANY DAYS HAS MY BABY TO PLAY?

How many days has my baby to play?
  Saturday, Sunday, Monday,
Tuesday, Wednesday, Thursday, Friday,
  Saturday, Sunday, Monday.

39

OVER THE FIELDS

Children walk in single file or with partners, reciting poem and keeping time to the rhythm of the verses.

Over the fields where the cornflowers grow,
Over the fields where the poppies blow,
Over the stile there's a way we know —
   Down to a rustling wood!

Over the fields where the daisies grow,
Over the bank where the willows blow,
Over the bridge there's a way we know —
   Down to a rippling brook!

Over the hills where the rainbows go,
Where golden gorse and brambles grow,
Over the hills there's a way we know —
   Down to a rolling sea!

Adeline White

A FINGER PLAY FOR A SNOWY DAY

I
This is how snowflakes play about,
Up in cloudland they dance in and out.

II
This is how they whirl down the street,
Powdering everybody they meet.

III
This is how they come fluttering down,
Whitening the roads, the fields, and the town.

IV
This is how snowflakes cover the trees,
Each branch and twig bends in the breeze.

V

This is how snowflakes blow in a heap,
Looking just like fleecy sheep.

VI

This is how they cover the ground,
Cover it thickly, with never a sound.

VII

This is how people shiver and shake
On a snowy morning when first they wake.

VIII

This is how snowflakes melt away
When the sun sends out his beams to play.

FIVE LITTLE BROTHERS

Five little brothers set out together
    To journey the live-long day,
In an odd little carriage, all made of leather,
    They hurried away, away —
One big brother and three quite small,
And one wee fellow, no size at all.

The carriage was dark and none too roomy,
    And they could not move about;
The five little brothers grew very gloomy,
    And the wee one began to pout;
Till the biggest one whispered: 'What do you say?
Let's leave the carriage and run away.'

So out they scampered, the five together,
    And off and away they sped.
When somebody found the carriage of leather,
    Oh, my! how she shook her head!
'Twas her little boy's shoe, as everyone knows,
And the five little brothers were five little toes!

Ella Wheeler Wilcox

THERE ARE BIG WAVES

There are big waves and little waves,
  Green waves and blue,
Waves you can jump over,
  Waves you dive thro',
Waves that rise up
  Like a great water wall,
Waves that swell softly
  And don't break at all,
Waves that can whisper,
  Waves that can roar,
And tiny waves that run at you
  Running on the shore.

Eleanor Farjeon

OUR MOTHER

Hundreds of stars in the pretty sky,
  Hundreds of shells on the shore together,
Hundreds of birds that go singing by,
  Hundreds of birds in the sunny weather.

Hundreds of dewdrops to greet the dawn,
  Hundreds of bees in the purple clover,
Hundreds of butterflies on the lawn,
  But only one mother the wide world over.

THE WOLF AND THE LAMBS

(A verse-speaking piece suitable for acting)

Wolf:

Little young lambs, oh! why do you stay
  Up in the bleak hills amid the snow?
I know a place where the fields are gay,
  Where sweet-stalked clovers and daisies grow!
Follow me, little lambs! Follow me, do!
And pleasant pastures I'll show to you!

Lambs:

Oh, Mr Wolf, how kind you are
    To offer us lambs such splendid things!
But, tell us, please, is it very far?
    We are lambs, not birds, for we have no wings,
And little legs tire, indeed they do!
So perhaps we had better not go with you!

Wolf:

Little young lambs, it is very near!
    Only a dozen steps away!
How cold it is and dreary here,
    But there it is sunshine all the day!
Follow me, little lambs! Follow me, do!
And pleasant pastures I'll show to you!

Lambs:

Oh, Mr Wolf, how kind you are,
    But our mother has told us not to go!
She says that such pastures may be too far,
    She says there are far worse things than snow!
In fact, Mr Wolf – we tell you true! —
She says there is nothing worse than you!

Ivy O. Eastwick

THREE DOGS

I know a dog called Isaac,
    Who begs for cake at tea;
He's fat and white and most polite,
    And belongs to Timothy.

I know a dog who carries
    His master's walking-stick:
He's old and slow, and his name is Joe,
    And *he* belongs to Dick.

I know a dog called Jacob,
    The best of all the three,
Sedate and wise, with nice brown eyes,
    And *he* belongs to Me.

E. C. Brereton

IN MY GARDEN

A Poem for Dramatization

In my little garden
  By the apple tree,
Daffodils are dancing —
  One – two – three!

In my little garden
  By the kitchen door,
Daisies red are smiling —
  Two – three – four!

In my little garden
  By the winding drive,
Roses bright are climbing —
  Three – four – five!

In my little garden
  By the pile of bricks,
Hollyhocks are growing —
  Four – five – six!

In my little garden
  Down in sunny Devon,
Violets are hiding —
  Five – six – seven!

In my little garden
  By the cottage gate,
Pansies gay are shining —
  Six – seven – eight!

Daffodils in golden gowns,
  Daisies all in red,
Hollyhocks so very tall
  By the garden shed,

Roses in the sunshine,
  Violets dewy bright,
Pansies smiling gaily —
  What a lovely sight!

IF I WERE AN APPLE

If I were an apple
  And grew upon a tree,
I think I'd fall down
  On a nice boy like me.

I wouldn't stay there,
  Giving nobody joy;
I'd fall down at once,
  And say, 'Eat me, my boy.'

THROUGH NURSERYLAND

Now, rocking horse! rocking horse! where shall we go?
The world's such a very big place, you must know,
That to see all its wonders, the wiseacres say,
'Twould take us together a year and a day.

Suppose we first gallop to Banbury Cross,
To visit that lady upon a white horse,
And see if it's true that her fingers and toes
Make beautiful music, wherever she goes.

Then knock at the door of the Old Woman's Shoe,
And ask if her wonderful house is on view,
And peep at the children, all tucked up in bed,
And beg for a taste of the broth without bread.

On poor Humpty-Dumpty we'll certainly call,
Perhaps we might help him to get back on his wall;
Spare two or three minutes to comfort the Kits
Who've been kept without pie, just for losing their mits.

A rush to Jack Horner's, then down a steep hill,
Not over and over, like poor Jack and Jill!
So, rocking horse! rocking horse! scamper away,
Or we'll never get back in a year and a day.

MRS INDIARUBBER DUCK

Mrs Indiarubber Duck,
  I like to see you float
Round and round my bath-tub
  Like a tiny sailing boat.

Mrs Indiarubber Duck,
  I like to see you sip
The lovely soapy water
  When you take your morning dip.

Mrs Indiarubber Duck,
  I stroke your shining back,
But oh! how splendid it would be
  If only you could quack.

D. Carter

THE LITTLE PIGGIES

Child: Where are you going, you little pig?
1st Pig: I'm leaving my mother, I'm growing so big!

Child: So big, young pig!
           So young, so big!
       What, leaving your mother, you foolish young pig!
       Where are you going, you little pig?

2nd Pig: I've got a new spade, and I'm going to dig.

Child: To dig, little pig!
           A little pig dig!
       Well, I never saw a pig with a spade that could dig!
       Where are you going, you little pig?

3rd Pig: Why, I'm going to have a nice ride in a gig.

Child: In a gig, little pig!
           What, a pig in a gig!
       Well, I never saw a pig ride in a gig!
       Where are you going, little pig?

4th Pig: I'm going to the barber's to buy a wig.

Child: A wig, little pig!
          A pig in a wig!
      Why, whoever before saw a pig in a wig?
      Where are you going, you little pig?

5th Pig: Why, I'm going to the ball to dance a fine jig.

Child: A jig, little pig!
          A pig dance a jig!
      Well, I never before saw a pig dance a jig!

                                        Thomas Hood

WHO LIKES THE RAIN?

'I,' said the duck. 'I call it fun,
For I have my pretty red rubbers on;
They make a little three-toed track
In the soft, cool mud – quack! quack!'

'I,' cried the dandelion, 'I,
My roots are thirsty, my buds are dry,'
And she lifted a tousled yellow head
Out of her green and grassy bed.

Sang the brook: 'I welcome every drop,
Come down, dear raindrops; never stop
Until a broad river you make of me,
And then I will carry you to the sea.'

'I,' shouted Ted, 'for I can run,
With my high-top boots and raincoat on,
Through every puddle and runlet and pool
I find on the road to school.'

OFF WE GO TO MARKET

1. We feed the chickens every day,
(*Action of feeding chickens.*)

Singing as we go.
(*Partners take hands and swing across to opposite positions.*)

We gather up the eggs they lay,
(*Action of picking up eggs.*)

Singing as we go.
(*Partners take hands and swing back to places.*)

Then off we go to market,
Off we go to market,
Off we go to market,
Singing as we go.
(*Still with hands across, all follow the first couple down the room and back to place.*)

2. We plant the turnips in the ground,
   Singing as we go.
We pull them when they're large and round,
   Singing as we go.
Then off we go to market,
Off we go to market,
Off we go to market,
   Singing as we go.

3. We gather cherries ripe and red,
   Singing as we go.
We put them in a basket bed,
   Singing as we go.
Then off we go to market,
Off we go to market,
Off we go to market,
   Singing as we go.

Gwen A. Smith

WHO?

Who will feed the dicky-birds on the garden wall?
Winter-time is very big – they are very small!

Who will feed the dicky-birds on the frozen trees?
Every little twitter means, 'Feed us, if you please!'

Who will feed the dicky-birds in the frost and snow?
See them on the chimney-pot – cuddled in a row!

Who will feed the dicky-birds till the days of spring?
Think of what they do for you and the songs they sing!

I will feed the dicky-birds, and when springtime comes,
Every little song will mean, 'Thank you for the crumbs!'

Florence Hoatson

TRAINS

Our garden's very near the trains;
   I think it's jolly fine
That I have just to climb the fence
   To watch the railway line!

I love to see the train that takes
   A minute to the mile;
The engine-man, as he goes past,
   Has only time to smile!

Then comes a train with empty trucks,
   That never goes so fast;
Its driver-man has always time
   To wave as he goes past!

The man who drives the luggage train,
   That passes here at three,
Not only smiles and waves his hand,
   But whistles once for me!

Hope Shepherd

MY LITTLE DOG

I helped a little lame dog
    Over such a stile,
He followed me with gratitude
    Many a weary mile.
I shoo-ed at him and chased him,
    But he stuck there, close behind;
(I'm sure his bark was saying,
    'I know that you'll be kind!')
He came into my housie,
    And he wouldn't go away,
So I'll keep my little lame dog
    To myself, if I may.

Pearl Forbes MacEwen

WHAT PIGGY-WIG FOUND

Piggy-wig found he had four little feet,
    And said to his mother one day,
'Mother, I find I have four little feet,
    What shall I do with them, pray?'

        'Run about, run about, Piggy-wig-wig,
        Run on your four little feet and grow big!'

Piggy-wig found he had two little eyes,
    And said to his mother one day,
'Mother, I find I have two little eyes,
    What shall I do with them, pray?'

        'Look about, look about, Piggy-wig-wig,
        Look with your two little eyes, and grow big!'

Piggy-wig found he had one little nose,
    And said to his mother one day,
'Mother, I find I have one little nose,
    What shall I do with it, pray?'

'Sniff about, sniff about, Piggy-wig-wig,
Sniff with your one little nose and grow big!'

Piggy-wig found he had one little mouth,
    And said to his mother one day,
'Mother, I find I have one little mouth,
    What shall I do with it, pray?'

        'Eat with it, eat with it, Piggy-wig-wig,
        Eat with your one little mouth and grow big!'

So Piggy-wig ran on his four little toes,
    And looked with his two little eyes,
And ate with his mouth, and sniffed with his nose,
    And soon he grew BIG and WISE!

                                        Enid Blyton

MAKING TENS

How many ways can you bring me ten?
Now think fast, my merry little men.

Glad to be first, see Jack's eyes shine,
As he quickly comes to me with one and —

Right on his heels his usual mate
Robert follows with two and —

Next to come is Dick from Devon,
And he has written three and —

Then follows quickly Harold Hicks,
I see he makes it four and —

Last of all comes Mortimer Clive,
But first to think of five and —

                                    M. M. Hutchinson

THE KING OF CHINA'S DAUGHTER

The King of China's daughter,
  So beautiful to see
With her face like yellow water, left
  Her nutmeg tree.
Her little rope for skipping
  She kissed and gave it me —
Made of painted notes of singing-birds
  And the fields of tea.
I skipped across the nutmeg grove,
  I skipped across the sea;
But neither sun nor moon, my dear,
  Has yet caught me.

Edith Sitwell

LITTLE TROTTY WAGTAIL

Little Trotty Wagtail, he went in the rain,
And twittering, tottering sideways he ne'er got straight again.
He stooped to get a worm, and looked up to get a fly,
And then he flew away ere his feathers they were dry.

Little Trotty Wagtail, he waddled in the mud,
And left his little footmarks, trample where he would.
He waddled in the water-pudge, and waggle went his tail,
And chirrup up his wings to dry upon the garden rail.

Little Trotty Wagtail, you nimble all about,
And in the dimpling water-pudge you waddle in and out;
Your home is nigh at hand, and in the warm pig-stye,
So, little Master Wagtail, I'll bid you a good-bye.

John Clare

TWICE

Twice one are two,
  And twice two are four,
Say it over carefully
  At least once more.

Twice two are four,
　And twice three are six,
Say it over carefully
　Until it sticks.

Twice three are six,
　And twice four are eight,
Write it down on paper, pad,
　Or on your slate.

Twice four are eight,
　And twice five are ten,
Write it down with pencil
　Or with chalk or pen.

Twice five are ten,
　And twice six are twelve,
In the number garden
　You must delve, delve, delve.

M. M. Hutchinson

MINCEMEAT

Sing a song of mincemeat,
　Currants, raisins, spice,
Apples, sugar, nutmeg,
　Everything that's nice,
Stir it with a ladle,
　Wish a lovely wish,
Drop it in the middle
　Of your well-filled dish,
Stir again for good luck,
　Pack it all away
Tied in little jars and pots,
　Until Christmas Day.

Elizabeth Gould

TWO LITTLE KITTENS

Two little kittens,
  One stormy night,
Began to quarrel,
  And then to fight.

One had a mouse
  And the other had none;
And that was the way
  The quarrel begun.

'I'll have that mouse,'
  Said the bigger cat.
'You'll have that mouse?
  We'll see about that!'

'I will have that mouse,'
  Said the tortoise-shell;
And, spitting and scratching,
  On her sister she fell.

I've told you before
  'Twas a stormy night,
When these two kittens
  Began to fight.

The old woman took
  The sweeping broom,
And swept them both
  Right out of the room.

The ground was covered
  With frost and snow,
They had lost the mouse,
  And had nowhere to go.

So they lay and shivered
  Beside the door,
Till the old woman finished
  Sweeping the floor.

And then they crept in
   As quiet as mice,
All wet with snow
   And as cold as ice.

They found it much better
   That stormy night,
To lie by the fire,
   Than to quarrel and fight.

Jane Taylor

TEN LITTLE INDIAN BOYS

One little Indian boy making a canoe,
Another came to help him and then there were two.

Two little Indian boys climbing up a tree,
They spied another one and then there were three.

Three little Indian boys playing on the shore,
They called another one and then there were four.

Four little Indian boys learning how to dive,
An older one taught them and then there were five.

Five making arrows then from slender shining sticks,
One came to lend a bow and then there were six.

Six little Indian boys wishing for eleven,
One only could they find and then there were seven.

Seven little Indian boys marched along in state,
One joined the growing line and then there were eight.

Eight little Indian boys camping near the pine,
One came with bait for fish and then there were nine.

Nine little Indian boys growing to be men,
Captured another brave and then there were ten.

M. M. Hutchinson

MICE

I think mice
Are rather nice.

Their tails are long,
Their faces small,
They haven't any
Chins at all.
Their ears are pink,
Their teeth are white,
They run about
The house at night.
They nibble things
They shouldn't touch
And no one seems
To like them much.

But I think mice
Are nice.

Rose Fyleman

STRANGE TALK

A little green frog lived under a log,
  And every time he spoke,
Instead of saying, 'Good morning,'
  He only said, 'Croak-croak.'

A duck lived by the waterside,
  And little did he lack,
But when we asked, 'How do you do?'
  He only said, 'Quack-quack.'

A rook lived in an elm tree,
  And all the world he saw,
But when he tried to make a speech
  It sounded like, 'Caw-caw.'

A little pig lived in a sty,
  As fat as he could be,
And when he asked for dinner
  He cried aloud, 'Wee-wee.'

Three pups lived in a kennel,
  And loved to make a row,
And when they meant, 'May we go out?'
  They said, 'Bow-wow! Bow-wow!'

If all these animals talked as much
  As little girls and boys,
And all of them tried to speak at once,
  Wouldn't it make a noise?

L. E. Yates

LITTLE LUCY LESTER

Little Lucy Lester was a funny little lady;
  Up the grassy meadow she would run with all her might;
When she reached the other end, she'd scamper back so gaily,
  Right into her little house where lived her cat so white.
'Why for do you run so fast?' said Farmer Giles in passing,
  'Are you going to catch a train, or is your white cat ill?'
'Neither, thank you kindly,' said that little Lucy Lester —
  'You see, I go by clock-work, and I can't stand still.'

M. Steel

THE FARMYARD

One black horse standing by the gate,
Two plump cats eating from a plate;
Three big goats kicking up their heels,
Four pink pigs full of grunts and squeals;
Five white cows coming slowly home,
Six small chicks starting off to roam;
Seven fine doves perched upon the shed,
Eight grey geese eager to be fed;
Nine young lambs full of frisky fun,
Ten brown bees buzzing in the sun.

A. A. Attwood

TOAD THE TAILOR

Toad the Tailor lived in a well,
   Croak! Croak! Croak! he would sing.
Instead of a knocker his door had a bell.
      Croak! C-C-C-Croak!

The bell, it was hung with the greatest of care,
   Croak! Croak! Croak! he would sing.
At the top of the steps leading down to him there,
      Croak! C-C-C-Croak!

By the light of a lantern his customers came,
   Croak! Croak! Croak! he would sing.
He measured them all by the length of their name.
      Croak! C-C-C-Croak!

But nobody grumbled a bit about that,
   Croak! Croak! Croak! he would sing.
It suited the thin and it suited the fat,
      Croak! C-C-C-Croak!

In time the old Toad grew as rich as could be,
   Croak! Croak! Croak! he would sing.
So he hung out a notice, 'All Tailoring Free.'
      Croak! C-C-C-Croak!

N. E. Hussey

LITTLE BROWN SEED

Little brown seed, round and sound,
Here I put you in the ground.

You can sleep a week or two,
Then – I'll tell you what to do:

You must grow some downward roots,
Then some tiny upward shoots.

From those green shoots' folded sheaves
Soon must come some healthy leaves.

When the leaves have time to grow
Next a bunch of buds must show.

Last of all, the buds must spread
Into blossoms white or red.

There, Seed! I've done my best.
Please to grow and do the rest.

Rodney Bennett

NOISES IN THE NIGHT

When I'm in bed at night,
All tucked up warm and tight,
All kinds of noises
Go in at my two ears.
Brr . . . go the motor-cars
Out on the street.
Whirr . . . sings the wind
As it blows round the house.
Ting-a-ling-ling
Ring the bicycle bells.
And ding-dong, ding-dong,
Sings the Grandfather Clock downstairs.
Then I hear nothing – nothing at all,
Because I'm asleep, sound asleep.

1. *Children pretend to cuddle down in bed.*
2. *They listen to the noises as the teacher tells the story.*
3. *They close their eyes and go fast asleep as the teacher very quietly and slowly says the last two lines.*

Lilian McCrea

THE MILKMAN

Clink, clink, clinkety-clink,
The milkman's on his rounds, I think.
Crunch, crunch, come the milkman's feet
Closer and closer along the street —
Then clink, clink, clinkety-clink,
He's left our bottles of milk to drink.

Clive Sansom

TEN LITTLE DICKY-BIRDS

(Addition in Ones to Ten)

1. One little dicky-bird
      Hopped on my shoe;
   Along came another one,
      And that made two.

Chorus:

      Fly to the tree-tops;
         Fly to the ground;
      Fly, little dicky-birds,
         Round and round.

2. Two little dicky-birds,
      Singing in a tree;
   Along came another one,
   And that made three.

Chorus

3. Three little dicky-birds,
      Came to my door;
   Along came another one,
      And that made four.

Chorus

4. Four little dicky-birds
      Perched on a hive;
   Along came another one,
   And that made five.

Chorus

5. Five little dicky-birds
      Nesting in the ricks;
   Along came another one,
   And that made six.

Chorus

6. Six little dicky-birds
      Flying up to heaven;
   Along came another one,
      And that made seven.

Chorus

7. Seven little dicky-birds
     Sat upon a gate;
   Along came another one,
     And that made eight.

                                    Chorus

8. Eight little dicky-birds
     Swinging on a line;
   Along came another one,
     And that made nine.

                                    Chorus

9. Nine little dicky-birds
     Looking at a hen;
   Along came another one,
     And that made ten.

                                    Chorus

Actions:
   Fingers are erected one by one from closed fists, to represent the birds. During the chorus, actions are as follows:
   Line 1. 'Birds' are held up high.
   Line 2. 'Birds' are held down low.
   Lines 3 and 4. 'Birds' are circled round and round.

                                    A. W. I. Baldwin

WANDERING JACK

Listen to the song
  Of Wandering Jack.
He carries a bundle
  On his back.
What is inside it?
  Shall I tell?
He carries inside it
  Dreams to sell.
Some cost a penny,
  Some cost a pound.
But some cost nothing,
  I'll be bound.

                                    Emile Jacot

MRS JENNY WREN

Mrs Jenny Wren!
  I have never, never heard
Such a very big voice
  For a very tiny bird.
You sit on a post
  And you sing and you sing,
You're a very bold bird
  For such a tiny little thing,
    Jenny Wren.

If I had a voice
  For my size as big as yours,
I should never dare sing
  Without shutting all the doors.
I'd sing very softly
  For fear they should hear,
Or they'd hurry away
  And put a finger in each ear,
    Jenny Wren.

Rodney Bennett

THE TWO FAMILIES

One summer I stayed
  On a farm, and I saw
A quaint little sight
  I had not seen before.

A cat and her kittens,
  And a sow and her troop
Of little pink pigs
  In one family group.

The mother cat came
  To be petted by me,
While I looked at her kittens
  So sooty and wee!

Like tiny black smuts,
  The two little dears
Contentedly slept
  Beside the sow's ears.

Till one kitten woke,
  And started to roam
On Mrs Pig's back
  As if quite at home.

And there it sat down
  To gaze at its friends,
The little pink pigs
  With their queer curly ends!

And old Mother Pig
  Snored loudly and deep,
Nor noticed the kittens,
  Awake or asleep!

Joyce L. Brisley

IN THE MIRROR

In the mirror
On the wall,
There's a face
I always see;
Round and pink,
And rather small,
Looking back again
At me.

It is very
Rude to stare,
But she never
Thinks of that,
For her eyes are
Always there;
What can she be
Looking at?

Elizabeth Fleming

A GROWING RHYME

A farmer once planted some little brown seeds
　　With a pit-a-pit, pit-a-pat, pit-a-pat, pat.
He watered them often and pulled up the weeds,
　　With a tug-tug at this and a tug-tug at that.
The little seeds grew tall and green in the sun,
　　With a push-push up here, and a push-push up there,
And a beautiful plant grew from every one,
　　With a hey diddle, holding their heads in the air.

J. M. Westrup

SONG FOR A BALL-GAME

Bounce ball! Bounce ball!
　　One – two – three.
Underneath my right leg
　　And round about my knee.
Bounce ball! Bounce ball!
　　Bird – or – bee
Flying from the rose-bud
　　Up into the tree.

Bounce ball! Bounce ball!
　　Fast – you – go
Underneath my left leg
　　And round about my toe.
Bounce ball! Bounce ball!
　　Butt – er – fly
Flying from the rose-bud
Up into the sky.

Bounce ball! Bounce ball!
　　You – can't – stop.
Right leg and left leg
　　Round them both you hop.
Bounce ball! Bounce ball!
　　Shy – white – dove,
Tell me how to find him,
　　My own true love.

Wilfred Thorley

64

Fantasy and Fairyland

PART TWO

We want to go to Fairyland
To dance by the light of the moon

THE RAINBOW FAIRIES

Two little clouds, one summer's day,
   Went flying through the sky;
They went so fast they bumped their heads,
   And both began to cry.

Old Father Sun looked out and said:
   'Oh, never mind, my dears,
I'll send my little fairy folk
   To dry your falling tears.'

One fairy came in violet,
   And one wore indigo;
In blue, green, yellow, orange, red,
   They made a pretty row.

They wiped the cloud-tears all away,
   And then from out the sky,
Upon a line the sunbeams made,
   They hung their gowns to dry.

I'D LOVE TO BE A FAIRY'S CHILD

Children born of fairy stock
Never need for shirt or frock,
Never want for food or fire,
Always get their heart's desire:
Jingle pockets full of gold,
Marry when they're seven years old,
Every fairy child may keep
Two strong ponies and ten sheep;
All have houses, each his own,
Built of brick or granite stone;
They live on cherries, they run wild —
I'd love to be a fairy's child.

Robert Graves

THE FAIRY FLUTE

My brother has a little flute
   Of gold and ivory,
He found it on a summer night
   Within a hollow tree,
He plays it every morning
   And every afternoon,
And all the little singing-birds
   Listen to the tune.

He plays it in the meadows,
   And everywhere he walks
The flowers start a-nodding
   And dancing on their stalks.

He plays it in the village,
   And all along the street
The people stop to listen,
   The music is so sweet.

And none but he can play it
   And none can understand,
Because it is a fairy flute
   And comes from Fairyland.

Rose Fyleman

THE LITTLE MEN

Would you see the little men
Coming down a moonlit glen? —
Gnome and elf and woodland sprite,
Clad in brown and green and white,
Skipping, hopping, never stopping,
Stumbling, grumbling, tumbling, mumbling,
Dancing, prancing, singing, swinging —
Coats of red and coats of brown,
Put on straight or upside-down,
Outside-in or inside-out,
Some with sleeves and some without,
Rustling, bustling, stomping, romping,
Strumming, humming, hear them coming —
You will see the Little Men
If it be a Fairy glen.

Flora Fearne

AN ELFIN KNIGHT

He put his acorn helmet on;
It was plumed of the silk of the thistledown;
The corselet plate that guarded his breast
Was once the wild bee's golden vest;
His cloak, of a thousand mingled dyes,
Was formed of the wings of butterflies;
His shield was the shell of a ladybird green,
Studs of gold on a ground of green;
And the quivering lance which he brandished bright,
Was the sting of a wasp he had slain in fight.

Swift he bestrode his firefly steed;
  He bared his blade of the bent-grass blue;
He drove his spurs of the cockle-seed,
  And away like a glance of thought he flew,
To skim the heavens, and follow far
The fiery trail of the rocket star.

John Rodman Drake

CHILD'S SONG

I know the sky will fall one day,
  The great green trees will topple down,
The spires will wither far away
  Upon the battlemented town;
When winds and waves forget to flow
  And the wild song-birds cease from calling,
Then shall I take my shoes and go
  To tell the King the sky is falling.

There's lots of things I've never done,
  And lots of things I'll never see;
The nearest rainbow ever spun
  Is much too far away from me;
But when the dark air's lost in snow
  And the long quiet strikes appalling,
I learn how it will feel to go
  To tell the King the sky is falling.

Gerald Gould

FAIRY FEET

Nobody lives in the cottage now,
  But birds build under the thatch,
And a trailing rose half hides the door
  And twines itself round the latch.

Nobody walks up the cobble path,
  Where the grass peeps in between,
But fairy feet tread the cobble stones
  And keep them wonderfully clean.

Nobody knows that the raindrops bright
  Which fall on the grey old stones
Are the feet of the fairies dancing for joy
  On the path that nobody owns.

Phyllis L. Garlick

A CHILD'S THOUGHT

At seven, when I go to bed,
I find such pictures in my head:
Castles with dragons prowling round,
Gardens where magic fruits are found;
Fair ladies prisoned in a tower,
Or lost in an enchanted bower;
While gallant horsemen ride by streams
That border all this land of dreams
I find, so clearly in my head
At seven, when I go to bed.

At seven, when I wake again,
The magic land I seek in vain;
A chair stands where the castle frowned,
The carpet hides the garden ground,
No fairies trip across the floor,
Boots, and not horsemen, flank the door,
And where the blue streams rippling ran
Is now a bath and water-can;
I seek the magic land in vain
At seven, when I wake again.

Robert Louis Stevenson

69

BUBBLES

Out in the garden
When school was done
I blew bubbles
In the sun.

I blew a bubble
Huge as could be!
It hung in the air
For all to see.

Into my bubble
I looked and found
A shining land
That was rainbow round.

It looked like a world
Meant for no one but fairies.
They'd keep little farms there
With cows, chicks, and dairies.
Woods where the pixies
Could picnic for pleasure,
And hide near the rainbows
Their crocks of strange treasure.

Countries were marked there
Plain as could be;
Green for the country,
Blue for the sea.
Purple for heather,
Sunshine like gold,
Bubble-land weather
Could never be cold.

And then came a bee
All furry and fat.
Before I could think
What he would be at
My beautiful bubble
He brushed with his wing,
And all that was left
Was a little damp ring.

L. Nicholson

THE DREAM FAIRY

A little fairy comes at night,
  Her eyes are blue, her hair is brown,
With silver spots upon her wings,
  And from the moon she flutters down.

She has a little silver wand,
  And when a good child goes to bed
She waves her wand from right to left
  And makes a circle round her head.

And then it dreams of pleasant things,
  Of fountains filled with fairy fish,
And trees that bear delicious fruit,
  And bow their branches at a wish;

Of arbours filled with dainty scents
  From lovely flowers that never fade,
Bright flies that glitter in the sun,
  And glow-worms shining in the shade;

And talking birds with gifted tongues
  For singing songs and telling tales,
And pretty dwarfs to show the way
  Through fairy hills and fairy dales.

Thomas Hood

A WISH

I'd love to give a party
  To all the fairy folk,
With scarlet autumn leaves for plates,
  Oh! it would be a joke!
And every little lady fay
  Should have her acorn cup,
To hold her fragrant rose-leaf tea,
  Until she drank it up;
And every little elf should have
  His acorn pipe to smoke;
I'd love to give a party
  Beneath this grand old oak.

Elizabeth Gould

ABOUT THE FAIRIES

Pray, where are the little bluebells gone,
    That lately blossomed in the wood?
Why, the little fairies have each taken one,
    And put it on for a hood.

And where are the pretty grass-stalks gone,
    That waved in the summer breeze?
Oh, the fairies have taken them, every one,
    To plant in their gardens like trees.

And where are the great big blue-bottles gone,
    That buzzed in their busy pride?
Oh, the fairies have caught them, every one,
    And have broken them in, to ride.

And they've taken the glow-worms to light their halls,
    And the cricket to sing them a song;
And the great red rose leaves to paper their walls,
    And they're feasting the whole night long.

And when Spring comes back, with its soft mild ray,
    And the ripple of gentle rain,
The fairies bring what they've taken away,
    And give it us all again.

Jean Ingelow

THE WAY TO FAIRYLAND

Which is the way to Fairyland,
To Fairyland, to Fairyland?
We want to go to Fairyland,
    To dance by the light of the moon.

Up the hill and down the lane,
Down the lane, down the lane,
Up the hill and down the lane,
    You'll get there very soon.

Across the common and through the gate,
Through the gate, through the gate,
Across the common and through the gate,
   You'll get there very soon.

Over the stile and into the wood,
Into the wood, into the wood,
Over the stile and into the wood,
   You'll get there very soon.

Here we are in Fairyland,
In fairyland, in Fairyland,
Here we are in Fairyland,
   We'll dance by the light of the moon.

Eunice Close

FAIRY MUSIC

I found a little fairy flute
   Beneath a harebell blue;
I sat me down upon the moss
   And blew a note or two.

And as I blew the rabbits came
   Around me in the sun,
And little mice and velvet moles
   Came creeping, one by one.

A swallow perched upon my head,
   A robin on my thumb,
The thrushes sang in tune with me,
   The bees began to hum.

I loved to see them all around
   And wished they'd always stay,
When down a little fairy flew
   And snatched my flute away!

And then the swallow fluttered off,
   And gone were all the bees,
The rabbits ran, and I was left
   Alone among the trees!

Enid Blyton

THE KIND MOUSE

There once was a cobbler,
  And he was so wee
That he lived in a hole
  In a very big tree.
He had a good neighbour,
  And she was a mouse —
She did his wee washing
  And tidied his house.

Each morning at seven
  He heard a wee tap,
And in came the mouse
  In her apron and cap.
She lighted his fire
  And she fetched a wee broom,
And she swept and she polished
  His little Tree-room.

To take any wages
  She'd always refuse,
So the cobbler said, 'Thank you!'
  And mended her shoes;
And the owl didn't eat her,
  And even the cat
Said, 'I *never* could catch
  A kind mousie like that!'

Natalie Joan

SEA FAIRIES

They're hiding by the pebbles,
  They're running round the rocks.
Each of them, and all of them
  In dazzling sea-green frocks.

They're gathering strips of seaweed,
  The ribands fair that lie
Along the winding water mark
  The tide has left so high.

They're flying with the sand,
    They're singing in the caves,
And dancing in the white foam
    They toss from off the waves.

But if you try to catch them
    They're always out of reach —
Not everywhere and anywhere,
    But somewhere on the beach.

Eileen Mathias

MRS BROWN

As soon as I'm in bed at night
    And snugly settled down,
The little girl I am by day
Goes very suddenly away,
    And then I'm Mrs Brown.

I have a family of six,
    And all of them have names,
The girls are Joyce and Nancy Maud,
The boys are Marmaduke and Claude
    And Percival and James.

We have a house with twenty rooms
    A mile away from town;
I think it's good for girls and boys
To be allowed to make a noise,
    And so does Mr Brown.

We do the most exciting things,
    Enough to make you creep,
And on and on and on we go,
I sometimes wonder if I know
    When I have gone to sleep.

Rose Fyleman

RUFTY AND TUFTY

Rufty and Tufty were two little elves
  Who lived in a hollow oak tree.
They did all the cooking and cleaning themselves
  And often asked friends in to tea.

Rufty wore blue, and Tufty wore red,
  And each had a hat with a feather.
Their best Sunday shoes they kept under the bed —
  They were made of magic green leather.

Rufty was clever and kept the accounts,
  But Tufty preferred to do cooking.
He could make a fine cake without weighing amounts —
  And eat it when no one was looking!

Isabell Hempseed

THE FAIRY SHOEMAKER

Tiny shoes so trim and neat,
Fairy shoes for dancing feet;
See the elfin cobbler's shelves
Filled with shoes for tiny elves.

　　And sitting there he hammers,
　　And hammering he sings. . . .

'This small shoe of silver,
  This small shoe of gold,
This small shoe of diamonds bright —
  Will none of them grow old.

'This small shoe will hurry,
  This small shoe will skip,
This small shoe will dance all night,
  Tipperty, tip, tip, tip.

'This small shoe will twinkle,
  This small shoe will shine,
This small shoe will bring me home,
  For I shall make it mine.'

And sitting there he hammers,
And hammering he dreams. . . .

Tiny shoes so trim and neat,
Fairy shoes for dancing feet,
See the elfin cobbler smile
As he sits and rests awhile.

Phyllis L. Garlick

THE GOBLIN

A goblin lives in our house, in our house, in our house,
A goblin lives in our house all the year round.

He bumps
And he jumps
And he thumps
And he stumps.
He knocks
And he rocks
And he rattles at the locks.

A goblin lives in our house, in our house, in our house,
A goblin lives in our house all the year round.

Rose Fyleman

THE MAGIC WHISTLE

On my little magic whistle I will play to you all day;
I will play you songs of Summer and the hilltops far away;
I will play you songs of Spring-time when the daffodillies bloom
And the wild March horses scamper by across the golden broom.

I will play you sweetest music of the silver fluttering trees,
When the raindrops gently falling touch the quivering autumn leaves;
I will play to you of castles 'neath a fairy sky of blue;
On my little magic whistle, oh! I'd play it all to you.

Margaret Rose

TOADSTOOLS

It's not a bit windy,
It's not a bit wet,
The sky is as sunny
As summer, and yet
Little umbrellas are
Everywhere spread,
Pink ones, and brown ones,
And orange, and red.

I can't see the folks
Who are hidden below;
I've peeped, and I've peeped
Round the edges, but no!
They hold their umbrellas
So tight and so close
That nothing shows under,
Not even a nose!

Elizabeth Fleming

A FAIRY SONG

Over hill, over dale,
Thorough bush, thorough brier,
Over park, over pale,
Thorough flood, thorough fire!
I do wander everywhere,
Swifter than the moon's sphere;
And I serve the fairy queen,
To dew her orbs upon the green:
The cowslips tall her pensioners be;
In their gold coats spots you see;
Those be rubies, fairy favours,
In those freckles live their savours:
I must go seek some dewdrops here,
And hang a pearl in every cowslip's ear.

Shakespeare

The Seasons, Flowers and Trees

PART THREE

Therefore all seasons shall be sweet to thee

WINTER AND SPRING

But a little while ago
All the ground was white with snow;
Trees and shrubs were dry and bare,
Not a sign of life was there;
Now the buds and leaves are seen,
Now the fields are fresh and green,
Pretty birds are on the wing,
With a merry song they sing!
There's new life in everything!
How I love the pleasant spring!

A CHANGE IN THE YEAR

It is the first mild day of March:
  Each minute sweeter than before,
The redbreast sings from the tall larch
  That stands beside our door.

There is a blessing in the air,
  Which seems a sense of joy to yield
To the bare trees, and mountains bare,
  And grass in the green field.

William Wordsworth

APRIL

April, April,
Laugh thy girlish laughter;
Then, the moment after,
Weep thy girlish tears!
April, that mine ears
Like a lover greetest,
If I tell thee, sweetest,
All my hopes and fears,
April, April,
Laugh thy golden laughter,
But, the moment after,
Weep thy golden tears.

Sir William Watson

THE FOUR SWEET MONTHS

First, April, she with mellow showers
Opens the way for early flowers;
Then after her comes smiling May,
In a more sweet and rich array;
Next enters June, and brings us more
Gems than those two that went before:
Then, lastly, July comes, and she
More wealth brings in than all those three.

Robert Herrick

MAY

I feel a newer life in every gale;
   The winds, that fan the flowers,
And with their welcome breathings fill the sail,
   Tell of serener hours —
      Of hours that glide unfelt away
      Beneath the sky of May.

The spirit of the gentle south-wind calls
   From his blue throne of air,
And where his whispering voice in music falls,
   Beauty is budding there;
      The bright ones of the valley break
      Their slumbers, and awake.

The waving verdure rolls along the plain,
   And the wide forest weaves,
To welcome back its playful mates again,
   A canopy of leaves;
      And from its darkening shadows floats
      A gush of trembling notes.

Fairer and brighter spreads the reign of May;
   The tresses of the woods
With the light dallying of the west-wind play;
   And the full-brimming floods,
      As gladly to their goal they run,
      Hail the returning sun.

J. G. Percival

SUMMER IS NIGH

Summer is nigh!
How do I know?
Why, this very day
A robin sat
On a tilting spray,
And merrily sang
A song of May.
Jack Frost has fled
From the rippling brook;
And a trout peeped out
From his shady nook.
A butterfly too
Flew lazily by,
And the willow catkins
Shook from on high
Their yellow dust
As I passed by:
And so I know
That summer is nigh.

THE BARREL ORGAN

Go down to Kew in lilac-time, in lilac-time, in lilac-time,
Go down to Kew in lilac-time (it isn't far from London!);
And you shall wander hand in hand with love in summer's wonderland;
Go down to Kew in lilac-time (it isn't far from London!).

The cherry trees are seas of bloom and soft perfume and sweet perfume,
The cherry trees are seas of bloom (and oh! so near to London!);
And there they say, when dawn is high, and all the world's a blaze of
sky,
The cuckoo, though he's very shy, will sing a song for London.

The nightingale is rather rare and yet they say you'll hear him there,
At Kew, at Kew, in lilac-time (and oh! so near to London!);
The linnet and the throstle, too, and after dark the long halloo,
And golden-eyed tu-whit, tu-whoo of owls that ogle London.

For Noah hardly knew a bird of any kind that isn't heard
At Kew, at Kew, in lilac-time (and oh! so near to London!);
And when the rose begins to pout, and all the chestnut spires are out,
You'll hear the rest without a doubt, all chorusing for London:

Come down to Kew in lilac-time, in lilac-time, in lilac-time,
Come down to Kew in lilac-time (it isn't far from London!);
And you shall wander hand in hand with love in summer's wonderland;
Come down to Kew in lilac-time (it isn't far from London!).

Alfred Noyes

JUNE

Month of leaves,
Month of roses;
Gardens full
Of dainty posies;
  Skies of blue,
  Hedgerows gay,
  Meadows sweet
  With the new-mown hay.

Flowery banks,
A-drone with bees,
Dreaming cattle
Under trees:
  Song-birds pipe
    A merry tune —
  This is summer,
  This is June.

Irene F. Pawsey

HAYTIME

It's Midsummer Day
And they're cutting the hay
Down in the meadow just over the way,
The children all run
For a frolic, and fun —
For haytime is playtime out in the sun.

It's Midsummer Day,
And they're making the hay
Down in the meadow all golden and gay,
They're tossing it high
Beneath the June sky,
And the hay rakes are spreading it out to dry.

Irene F. Pawsey

MIDSUMMER NIGHT

The sun goes down,
  The stars peep out,
And long slim shadows
  Flit about.

In velvet shoes
  The quiet dark
Comes stepping soft
  O'er wood and park.

And now the world
  Is fast asleep;
And fays and elves
  Their revels keep.

They fly on the backs of the grey-winged moths,
  They skim on the dragon-flies green and gold.
On shimmering dew-wet grass they alight,
  Tiny petal-skirts whirl, gauzy wings unfold.

The fairies are dancing beneath the moon.
Hush! See the shimmer of their twinkling shoon!

Elizabeth Gould

AUGUST

The wind sang to the cornfields
  A happy little song,
And this is what he whispered,
  'The harvest won't be long.'

The wind sang to the windmill
  A merry little tune.
The windmill answered gaily,
  'The harvest's coming soon.'

The whispering of the poppies
  Through the cornfields steals along,
They are joining with the fairies
  Singing harvest's merry song.

Eunice Fallon

AUTUMN

I love the fitful gust that shakes
  The casement all the day,
And from the glossy elm tree takes
  The faded leaves away,
Twirling them by the window-pane
With thousand others down the lane.

I love to see the shaking twig
  Dance till shut of eve,
The sparrow on the cottage rig,
  Whose chirp would make believe
That Spring was just now flirting by
In Summer's lap with flowers to lie.

I love to see the cottage smoke
  Curl upwards through the trees;
The pigeons nestled round the cote
  On November days like these;
The cock upon the dunghill crowing,
The mill sails on the heath a-going.

John Clare

SEPTEMBER

There are twelve months throughout the year,
  From January to December —
And the primest month of all the twelve
  Is the merry month of September!
      Then apples so red
      Hang overhead,
      And nuts ripe-brown
      Come showering down
  In the bountiful days of September!

There are flowers enough in the summer-time,
  More flowers than I can remember —
But none with the purple, gold, and red
  That dye the flowers of September!
  The gorgeous flowers of September!
      And the sun looks through
      A clearer blue,
      And the moon at night
      Sheds a clearer light
  On the beautiful flowers of September!

The poor too often go scant and bare,
  But it glads my soul to remember
That 'tis harvest-time throughout the land
  In the bountiful month of September!
  Oh! the good, kind month of September!
      It giveth the poor
      The growth of the moor;
      And young and old
      'Mong sheaves of gold
  Go gleaning in rich September!

Mary Howitt

HARVEST SONG

The boughs do shake and the bells do ring,
So merrily comes our harvest in,
Our harvest in, our harvest in,
So merrily comes our harvest in.

We have ploughed, we have sowed,
We have reaped, we have mowed,
We have brought home every load,
Hip, hip, hip, harvest home!

RED IN AUTUMN

Tipperty-Toes, the smallest elf,
Sat on a mushroom by himself,
Playing a little tinkling tune
Under the big round harvest moon;
And this is the song that Tipperty made
To sing to the little tune he played.

'Red are the hips, red are the haws,
Red and gold are the leaves that fall,
Red are the poppies in the corn,
Red berries on the rowan tall;
Red is the big round harvest moon,
And red are my new little dancing shoon.'

Elizabeth Gould

OCTOBER

I've brought you nuts and hops;
And when the leaf drops, why, the walnut drops.
Crack your first nut and light your first fire,
Roast your first chestnut crisp on the bar;
Make the logs sparkle, stir the blaze higher,
Logs are as cheery as sun or as star,
Logs we can find wherever we are.
Spring one soft day will open the leaves,
Spring one bright day will lure back the flowers;
Never fancy my whistling wind grieves,
Never fancy I've tears in my showers:
Dance, night and days! and dance on, my hours!

Christina Rossetti

JACK FROST IN THE GARDEN

Jack Frost was in the garden;
  I saw him there at dawn;
He was dancing round the bushes
  And prancing on the lawn.
He had a cloak of silver,
  A hat all shimm'ring white,
A wand of glittering star-dust,
  And shoes of sunbeam light.

Jack Frost was in the garden,
  When I went out to play
He nipped my toes and fingers
  And quickly ran away.
I chased him round the wood-shed,
  But, oh! I'm sad to say
That though I chased him everywhere
  He simply wouldn't stay.

Jack Frost was in the garden:
  But now I'd like to know
Where I can find him hiding;
  I've hunted high and low —
I've lost his cloak of silver,
  His hat all shimm'ring white,
His wand of glittering star-dust,
  His shoes of sunbeam light.

John P. Smeeton

THERE'S SNOW ON THE FIELDS

There's snow on the fields,
  And cold in the cottage,
While I sit in the chimney nook
  Supping hot pottage.

My clothes are soft and warm,
  Fold upon fold,
But I'm so sorry for the poor
  Out in the cold.

Christina Rossetti

WINTER'S SONG

Drop down, drop down, white snowflakes!
We shall hide ourselves in fur coats
And when the blizzard comes
We shall put on fur caps,
We shall harness our golden sleighs,
We shall drive down from our hillside
And if we fall into a snowdrift
We hope that the wind will not cover us,
So that we can drive back quickly
For the fairy tales which grandfather will tell us.

(Translation from the Bohemian)

WHITE FIELDS

In winter-time we go
Walking in the fields of snow;

Where there is no grass at all;
Where the top of every wall,

Every fence, and every tree,
Is as white as white can be.

Pointing out the way we came —
Every one of them the same —

All across the fields there be
Prints in silver filigree;

And our mothers always know,
By the footprints in the snow,

Where it is the children go.

James Stephens

WINTER

O Winter's a beautiful time of the year.
There's frost on the hills,
There's snow in the air.
The buds are all still,
The boughs are all bare.

This little maid of long ago
Is warmly dressed from top to toe.
Her hands are hidden in her muff,
I wonder if she's warm enough!

Enid Blyton

IN THE WOOD

Cold winter's in the wood,
I saw him pass
Crinkling up fallen leaves
Along the grass.

Bleak winter's in the wood,
The birds have flown
Leaving the naked trees
Shivering alone.

King Winter's in the wood,
I saw him go
Crowned with a coronet
Of crystal snow.

Eileen Mathias

APPLE BLOSSOMS

Is there anything in Spring so fair
As apple blossoms falling through the air?

When from a hill there comes a sudden breeze
That blows freshly through all the orchard trees.

The petals drop in clouds of pink and white,
Noiseless like snow and shining in the light.

Making beautiful an old stone wall,
Scattering a rich fragrance as they fall.

There is nothing I know of to compare
With apple blossoms falling through the air.

Helen Adams Parker

PINK ALMOND

So delicate, so airy,
   The almond on the tree,
Pink stars that some good fairy
   Has made for you and me.

A little cloud of roses,
   All in a world of grey,
The almond flower uncloses
   Upon the wild March day.

A mist of roses blowing
   The way of fog and sleet,
A dust of roses showing
   For grey dust in the street.

Pink snow upon the branches,
   Pink snowflakes falling down
In rosy avalanches,
   Upon the dreary town.

A rain, a shower of roses,
   All in a roseless day,
The almond tree uncloses
   Her roses on the grey.

Katharine Tynan

MARIGOLDS

Do you like marigolds?
  If you do
Then my garden is
  Gay for you!

I've been cutting their
  Fragrant stalks
Where they lean on
  The garden walks.

The head's too heavy for
  The brittle stem,
A careless touch and
  You've broken them.

Each one shines like a
  Separate star
Set in some heaven where
  Gardens are.

My hands smell of the
  Herb-like scent,
Telling what garden
  Way I went.

Pungent, vivid and
  Strong, they stay
Long after Summer has
  Gone away.

Do you like marigolds?
  Here's a pledge
To meet the frost with
  A golden edge —

To go as far as
  A weak thing may
Linking tomorrow with
  Yesterday.

Louis Driscoll

BLUEBELLS

In the bluebell forest
   There is scarce a sound,
Only bluebells growing
   Everywhere around.

I can't see a blackbird
   Or a thrush to sing,
I think I can almost
   Hear the bluebells ring.

Ah! there is a bunny,
   And he's listening too,
Or perhaps he's thinking —
   What a sea of blue!

Olive Enoch

CHILD'S SONG IN SPRING

The silver birch is a dainty lady,
   She wears a satin gown;
The elm-tree makes the churchyard shady,
   She will not live in town.

The English oak is a sturdy fellow;
   He gets his green coat late;
The willow is smart in a suit of yellow,
   While brown the beech trees wait.

Such a gay green gown God gives the larches —
   As green as He is good!
The hazels hold up their arms for arches
   When Spring rides through the wood.

The chestnut's proud, and the lilac's pretty,
   The poplar's gentle and tall,
But the plane tree's kind to the poor dull city —
   I love him best of all!

E. Nesbit

93

CHERRY TREE

The Chaffinch flies fast
　　To the red cherry tree,
And sings as he goes:
　　'All for me! All for me!'

The Speckled Brown Thrush
　　Upon fluttering wing
Goes flying and scolds:
　　'Greedy thing! Greedy thing!'

The chattering Starling
　　He visits there, too,
And cries as he flies:
　　'Leave a few! Leave a few!'

But the Blackbird retreats
　　As the others advance,
And calls to them, laughing:
　　'Not a chance! Not a chance!'

Ivy O. Eastwick

CROCUSES

A kind voice calls, 'Come, little ones,
　　'Tis time to wake from sleeping!'
And out of bed without a word
　　The drowsy folk come creeping,
And soon above the chilly earth
　　Their tiny heads are peeping.

They bravely face the wind of March,
　　Its bite and bluster scorning
Like little soldiers – till, oh joy!
　　With scarce a word of warning
The crocuses slip off their caps
　　And give us gay good morning.

Anna M. Platt

From THE DAISY

There is a flower, a little flower,
  With silver crest and golden eye,
That welcomes every changing hour,
  And weathers every sky.

It smiles upon the lap of May,
  To sultry August spreads its charms,
Lights pale October on his way,
  And twines December's arms.

But this bold flowerlet climbs the hill,
  Hides in the forest, haunts the glen,
Plays on the margin of the rill,
  Peeps round the fox's den.

On waste and woodland, rock and plain,
  It's humble buds unheeded rise;
The Rose has but a summer reign,
  The Daisy never dies.

James Montgomery

BUTTERCUPS AND DAISIES

Buttercups and daisies,
  Oh, the pretty flowers;
Coming ere the spring-time,
  To tell of sunny hours,
While the trees are leafless,
  While the fields are bare,
Buttercups and daisies
  Spring up here and there.

Ere the snowdrop peepeth,
  Ere the crocus bold,
Ere the early primrose
  Opes its paly gold —
Somewhere on the sunny bank
  Buttercups are bright;
Somewhere 'mong the frozen grass
  Peeps the daisy white.

Mary Howitt

POPPIES

The strange, bright dancers
Are in the garden.
The wind of summer
Is a soft music.
Scarlet and orange,
Flaming and golden,
The strange, bright dancers
Move to the music.
And some are whiter
Than snow in winter,
And float like snowflakes
Drifting the garden.
Oh, have you seen them,
The strange, bright dancers,
Nodding and swaying
To the wind's music?

P. A. Ropes

TREES

The Oak is called the King of Trees,
The Aspen quivers in the breeze,
The Poplar grows up straight and tall,
The Pear tree spreads along the wall,
The Sycamore gives pleasant shade,
The Willow droops in watery glade,
The Fir tree useful timber gives,
The Beech amid the forest lives.

Sara Coleridge

PIMPERNEL

I'm the pert little pimpernel,
Who ever so cleverly weather foretells;
If I open my eye,
There's a cloudless sky;
If I shut it again,
Then it's sure to rain.

Charlotte Druitt Cole

THE FORGET-ME-NOT

When to the flowers so beautiful
   The Father gave a name,
Back came a little blue-eyed one
   (All timidly it came);
And standing at its Father's feet,
   And gazing in His face,
It said in low and trembling tones,
   And with a modest grace.
'Dear God, the name Thou gavest me,
   Alas! I have forgot.'
Kindly the Father looked Him down,
   And said, 'Forget Me Not.'

SNOWDROPS

I like to think
   That, long ago,
There fell to earth
   Some flakes of snow
Which loved this cold,
   Grey world of ours
So much, they stayed
   As snowdrop flowers.

Mary Vivian

VIOLETS

I know, blue modest violets
   Gleaming with dew at morn —
I know the place you come from
   And the way that you are born!

When God cut holes in heaven —
   The holes the stars look through —
He let the scraps fall down to earth;
   The little scraps are you!

FOXGLOVES

The foxglove bells, with lolling tongue,
Will not reveal what peals were rung
In Faery, in Faery,
A thousand ages gone.
All the golden clappers hang
As if but now the changes rang;
Only from the mottled throat
Never any echoes float.
Quite forgotten, in the wood,
Pale, crowded steeples rise;

All the time that they have stood
None has heard their melodies,
Deep, deep in wizardry
All the foxglove belfries stand.
Should they startle over the land,
None would know what bells they be.
Never any wind can ring them,
Nor the great black bees that swing them —
Every crimson bell, down-slanted,
Is so utterly enchanted.

Mary Webb

LEAVES

Leaves are always beautiful, I think.
At first they part their baby lips to drink
The rain in Spring, then open wider still,
Hungry for sweet winds and the sun, until
They lift their faces to the Summer rain,
Whose heavy drops pit-patter loud and plain.
The Autumn comes upon them and they change,
Decked out in glorious colours, rich and strange.
Then in the Winter they come flying down
Light as a breath, and crisp, and brown.
They fly before the wind like little elves,
And oh, I know they must enjoy themselves.

J. M. Westrup

PROUD LITTLE SPRUCE FIR

On a cold winter day the snow came down
  To cover the leafless trees,
Very glad they were of a snow-white gown,
  To keep out the chilly breeze.

But a little spruce fir, all gaily dressed
  In tiny sharp leaves of green,
Was drooping beneath the load on its breast,
  And not a leaf could be seen.

'I'm an evergreen tree,' he proudly thought,
  'And really they ought to know
That I'm looking my best, and care not a jot
  How bitter the wind may blow.'

Jeannie Kirby

TALL TREES

With their feet in the earth
  And their heads in the sky
The tall trees watch
  The clouds go by.

When the dusk sends quickly
  The birds to rest,
The tall trees shelter them
  Safe in a nest.

And then in the night
  With the tall trees peeping,
The moon shines down
  On a world that's sleeping.

Eileen Mathias

CHESTNUT BUDS

I have a mackintosh shiny brown,
To keep me warm when the rain pours down,
And the baby buds on the chestnut tree
Have shiny brown coverings, just like me.
For they've waited all through the frost and snow
For the Spring to come and the Winter to go;
That's why they've wrapped up so cosily,
Those little brown buds on the chestnut tree.

Evelyn M. Williams

THE SECRET JOY

Face to face with the sunflower,
  Cheek to cheek with the rose,
We follow a secret highway
  Hardly a traveller knows.
The gold that lies in the folded bloom
  Is all our wealth;
We eat of the heart of the forest
  With innocent stealth.
We know the ancient roads
  In the leaf of a nettle,
And bathe in the blue profound
  Of a speedwell petal.

Mary Webb

Out and About

PART FOUR

It is good to be out on the road, and going one knows not where

LEISURE

What is this life if, full of care,
We have no time to stand and stare?

No time to stand beneath the boughs
And stare as long as sheep or cows.

No time to see, when woods we pass,
Where squirrels hide their nuts in grass.

No time to see, in broad daylight,
Streams full of stars, like skies at night.

No time to turn at Beauty's glance,
And watch her feet, how they can dance.

No time to wait till her mouth can
Enrich that smile her eyes began.

A poor life this if, full of care,
We have no time to stand and stare.

W. H. Davies

THE RAIN

I hear leaves drinking Rain;
  I hear rich leaves on top
Giving the poor beneath
  Drop after drop;
'Tis a sweet noise to hear
These green leaves drinking near.

And when the Sun comes out,
  After this Rain shall stop,
A wondrous Light will fill
  Each dark, round drop;
I hope the Sun shines bright:
'Twill be a lovely sight.

W. H. Davies

PUPPY AND I

I met a Man as I went walking;
We got talking,
Man and I.
'Where are you going to, Man?' I said
  (I said to the Man as he went by).
'Down to the village, to get some bread.
  Will you come with me?' 'No, not I.'

I met a Horse as I went walking;
We got talking,
Horse and I.
'Where are you going to, Horse, today?'
  (I said to the Horse as he went by).
'Down to the village to get some hay.
  Will you come with me?' 'No, not I.'

I met a Woman, as I went walking;
We got talking,
Woman and I.
'Where are you going to, Woman, so early?'
  (I said to the Woman as she went by).
'Down to the village to get some barley.
  Will you come with me?' 'No, not I.'

I met some Rabbits as I went walking;
We got talking,
Rabbits and I.
'Where are you going in your brown fur coats?'
  (I said to the Rabbits as they went by).
'Down to the village to get some oats.
  Will you come with us?' 'No, not I.'

I met a Puppy as I went walking;
We got talking,
Puppy and I.
'Where are you going this nice fine day?'
  (I said to the Puppy as he went by).
'Up in the hills to roll and play.'
   'I'll come with you, Puppy,' said I.

A. A. Milne

TEWKESBURY ROAD

It is good to be out on the road, and going one knows not where,
  Going through meadow and village, one knows not whither nor why;
Through the grey light drift of the dust, in the keen cool rush of the air,
  Under the flying white clouds, and the broad blue lift of the sky.

And to halt at the chattering brook, in the tall green fern at the brink
  Where the harebell grows, and the gorse, and the foxgloves purple
    and white;
Where the shy-eyed delicate deer come down in a troop to drink
  When the stars are mellow and large at the coming on of the night.

O, to feel the beat of the rain, and the homely smell of the earth,
  Is a tune for the blood to jig to, a joy past power of words;
And the blessed green comely meadows are all a-ripple with mirth
  At the noise of the lambs at play and the dear wild cry of the birds.

John Masefield

MADRIGAL

Come let's begin to revel 't out,
And tread the hills and dales about,
That hills and dales and woods may sound
An echo to this warbling sound:
Fa la la la.

Lads merry be with music sweet,
And Fairies trip it with your feet,
Pan's pipe is dull; a better strain
Doth stretch itself to please your vein:
Fa la la la.

ROADWAYS

One road leads to London,
  One road runs to Wales,
My road leads me seawards
  To the white dipping sails.

One road leads to the river,
  As it goes singing slow;
My road leads to shipping,
  Where the bronzed sailors go.

Leads me, lures me, calls me
  To salt, green, tossing sea;
A road without earth's road-dust
  Is the right road for me.

A wet road, heaving, shining,
  And wild with seagulls' cries,
A mad salt sea-wind blowing
  The salt spray in my eyes.

My road calls me, lures me
  West, east, south, and north;
Most roads lead men homewards,
  My road leads me forth.

To add more miles to the tally
  Of grey miles left behind,
In quest of that one beauty
  God put me here to find.

John Masefield

SUNSET

The summer sun is sinking low;
  Only the tree-tops redden and glow;
Only the weather-cock on the spire
Of the village church is a flame of fire;
  All is in shadow below.

H. W. Longfellow

THE SILVER ROAD

Last night I saw a Silver Road
  Go straight across the Sea;
And quick as I raced along the Shore,
  That quick Road followed me.

It followed me all round the Bay,
  Where small Waves danced in tune;
And at the end of the Silver Road
  There hung a Silver Moon.

A large round Moon on a pale green Sky,
  With a Pathway bright and broad;
Some night I shall bring that Silver Moon
  Across that Silver Road!

Hamish Hendry

THE EARLY MORNING

The moon on the one hand, the dawn on the other:
The moon is my sister, the dawn is my brother.
The moon on my left and the dawn on my right.
My brother, good morning: my sister, good night.

Hilaire Belloc

THE WOOD OF FLOWERS

I went to the Wood of Flowers,
  (No one was with me)
I was there alone for hours;
  I was as happy as could be
In the Wood of Flowers.

There was grass on the ground,
  There were buds on the tree,
And the wind had a sound
  Of such gaiety,
That I was as happy,
  As happy could be,
In the Wood of Flowers.

James Stephens

106

THE PEDLAR'S CARAVAN

I wish I lived in a caravan,
With a horse to drive, like a pedlar-man!
Where he comes from nobody knows,
Nor where he goes to, but on he goes.

His caravan has windows two,
With a chimney of tin that the smoke comes through,
He has a wife, and a baby brown,
And they go riding from town to town.

Chairs to mend and delf to sell —
He clashes the basins like a bell.
Tea-trays, baskets, ranged in order,
Plates, with the alphabet round the border.

The roads are brown, and the sea is green,
But his house is just like a bathing-machine.
The world is round, but he can ride,
Rumble, and splash to the other side.

With the pedlar-man I should like to roam,
And write a book when I come home.
All the people would read my book,
Just like the Travels of Captain Cook.

W. B. Rands

SUN AND MOON

The moon shines clear as silver,
    The sun shines bright like gold,
And both are very lovely,
    And very, very old.

God hung them up as lanterns,
    For all beneath the sky;
And nobody can blow them out,
    For they are up too high.

Charlotte Druitt Cole

GO OUT

Go out
When the wind's about;
Let him buffet you
Inside out.

Go out
In a rainy drizzle;
Never sit by the fire
To sizzle.

Go out
When the snowflakes play;
Toss them about
On the white highway.

Go out
And stay till night;
When the sun is shedding
Its golden light.

Eileen Mathias

I WONDER

I wonder why the grass is green,
And why the wind is never seen?

Who taught the birds to build a nest,
And told the trees to take a rest?

O, when the moon is not quite round,
Where can the missing bit be found?

Who lights the stars, when they blow out,
And makes the lightning flash about?

Who paints the rainbow in the sky,
And hangs the fluffy clouds so high?

Why is it now, do you suppose,
That Dad won't tell me, if he knows?

Jeannie Kirby

SUCH A BLUSTERY DAY!

A merry wind danced over the hill,
    A madcap wind,
He shook the daffodil's golden crown,
And ruffled the clover's creamy gown;
Then off he sped, with a laughing shout,
To blow the hurrying clouds about,
And bustling back to earth again
He blew my bonnet all down the lane;

Then he hid behind a tree,
And pounced on me,

He blew me behind,
He blew me before,
He blew me right through the schoolroom door.

Elizabeth Gould

HALF HOLIDAY

What shall I do this afternoon?
Shall I go down to the river soon?
Or to the field where kingcups grow?
Or sail my kite if the breezes blow?

What shall I do that's best of all?
And shall I take my ship or ball?
For there are plenty of things to do,
The sunbeams dance and skies are blue.

P'r'aps I might hear the cuckoo sing,
Or find a new-grown fairy ring,
I saw a squirrel once over the hill,
P'r'aps he'd come out if I sat still.

What shall I do? Where shall I go?
See how the yellow gorse is a-glow,
All things are lovely that I see,
I'll follow this happy bumble-bee.

Olive Enoch

IN THE WOODS

Oh where have you been all the day
That you have been so long away?
Oh, I have been a woodland child,
And walked alone in places wild,
Bright eyes peered at me everywhere,
And voices filled the evening air;
All sounds of furred and feathered things,
The footfall soft, the whirr of wings,
Oh, I have seen grey squirrels play
At hide-and-seek the live-long day;
And baby rabbits full of fun
Poked out their noses in the sun,
And, unafraid, played there with me
In that still place of greenery.
A thousand secrets I have heard
From every lovely feathered bird;
The little red and yellow leaves
Danced round me in the autumn breeze,
In merry frolic to and fro,
As if they would not let me go.
How can I stay in this full town,
When those far woods are green and brown?

Dorothy Baker

WILD THYME

On the high hill pastures
  The west wind blows,
And little ones are dancing
  Where wild thyme grows.

Children and fairies
  Have dreams to keep,
Where wild thyme blossoms
  And old folk sleep.

Joyce Sambrook

LAUGHING SONG

When the green woods laugh with the voice of joy,
And the dimpling stream runs laughing by;
When the air does laugh with our merry wit,
And the green hill laughs with the noise of it;

When the meadows laugh with lively green,
And the grasshopper laughs in the merry scene;
When Mary, and Susan, and Emily
With their sweet round mouths sing, 'Ha, ha, he!'

When the painted birds laugh in the shade,
When our table with cherries and nuts is spread:
Come live, and be merry, and join with me,
To sing the sweet chorus of 'Ha, ha, he!'

William Blake

THE CITY CHILD

Dainty little maiden, whither would you wander?
  Whither from this pretty home, the home where mother dwells?
'Far and far away,' said the dainty little maiden,
  'All among the gardens, auriculas, anemones,
  Roses and lilies and Canterbury-bells.'

Dainty little maiden, whither would you wander?
  Whither from this pretty house, this city-house of ours?
'Far and far away,' said the dainty little maiden,
  'All among the meadows, the clover and the clematis,
  Daisies and kingcups and honeysuckle-flowers.'

Lord Tennyson

THE WIND IN THE GRASS

The green grass is bowing,
  The morning wind is in it,
'Tis a tune worth thy knowing,
  Though it change every minute.

Ralph W. Emerson

THE SCARECROW

A scarecrow stood in a field one day,
Stuffed with straw,
Stuffed with hay;
He watched the folk on the king's highway,
But never a word said he.

Much he saw, but naught did heed,
Knowing not night,
Knowing not day,
For, having nought, did nothing need,
And never a word said he.

A little grey mouse had made its nest,
Oh so wee,
Oh so grey,
In a sleeve of a coat that was poor Tom's best,
But the scarecrow naught said he.

His hat was the home of a small jenny wren,
Ever so sweet,
Ever so gay,
A squirrel had put by his fear of men,
And kissed him, but naught heeded he.

Ragged old man, I loved him well,
Stuffed with straw,
Stuffed with hay,
Many's the tale that he could tell,
But never a word says he.

Michael Franklin

THE GALLANT SHIP

Upon the gale she stooped her side,
And bounded o'er the swelling tide,
As she were dancing home;
The merry seamen laughed to see
Their gallant ship so lustily
Furrow the sea-green foam.

Sir Walter Scott

THE SONG OF THE GRASS

Here I come creeping, creeping everywhere;
    By the dusty road-side,
    On the sunny hill-side,
    Close by the noisy brook,
    In every shady nook,
I come creeping, creeping everywhere.

Here I come creeping, creeping everywhere;
    All around the open door,
    Where sit the agèd poor,
    Here where the children play,
    In the bright and merry May,
I come creeping, creeping everywhere.

Here I come creeping, creeping everywhere;
    You cannot see me coming,
    Nor hear my low, sweet humming;
    For in the starry night,
    And the glad morning light,
I come quietly creeping everywhere.

Here I come creeping, creeping everywhere;
    More welcome than the flowers,
    In Summer's pleasant hours;
    The gentle cow is glad,
    And the merry bird not sad,
To see me creeping, creeping everywhere.

Leigh Hunt

THE WIND

What way does the Wind come? What way does he go?
He rides over the water, and over the snow,
Through wood and through vale: and o'er rocky height
Which goat cannot climb, takes his sounding flight.
He tosses about in every bare tree,
As, if you look up, you plainly may see;
But how he will come, and whither he goes,
There's never a scholar in England knows.

Dorothy Wordsworth

PEBBLES

Pebbles, pebbles, pebbles,
  For miles and miles and miles:
A sloping bank of pebbles
  Round all the British Isles.

Grinding, grinding, grinding,
  Where the heavy billows pound,
Till they are smooth as marbles,
  And often just as round.

White ones, grey ones, brown ones,
  Lime and slate and quartz;
Yellow ones and pink ones,
  Pebbles of all sorts.

Tinkle, tinkle, tinkle,
  How strange it is to think
That after all these ages
  In my tin pail they clink.

Jewels, jewels, jewels
  For every child like me.
Oh, how I love the pebbles,
  Beside the sounding sea.

Edith King

THE CLIFF-TOP

The cliff-top has a carpet
  Of lilac, gold and green:
The blue sky bounds the ocean,
  The white clouds scud between.

A flock of gulls are wheeling
  And wailing round my seat;
Above my head the heaven,
  The sea beneath my feet.

Robert Bridges

DAY

'I am busy,' said the sea.
'I am busy. Think of me,
Making continents to be,
I am busy,' said the sea.

'I am busy,' said the rain.
'When I fall, it's not in vain;
Wait and you will see the grain.
I am busy,' said the rain.

'I am busy,' said the air.
'Blowing here and blowing there,
Up and down and everywhere.
I am busy,' said the air.

'I am busy,' said the sun,
'All my planets, every one,
Know my work is never done.
I am busy,' said the sun.

Sea and rain and air and sun,
Here's a fellow toiler: – one
Whose task will soon be done.

Sir Cecil Spring-Rice

IS THE MOON TIRED?

Is the moon tired? She looks so pale
Within her misty veil;
She scales the sky from east to west,
And takes no rest.

Before the coming of the night
The moon shows papery white;
Before the dawning of the day,
She fades away.

Christina Rossetti

THE RIVALS

I heard a bird at dawn
　Singing sweetly on a tree,
That the dew was on the lawn,
　And the wind was on the lea;
But I didn't listen to him,
　For he didn't sing to me!

I didn't listen to him,
　For he didn't sing to me
That the dew was on the lawn,
　And the wind was on the lea!
I was singing at the time,
　Just as prettily as he!

I was singing all the time,
　Just as prettily as he,
About the dew upon the lawn,
　And the wind upon the lea!
So I didn't listen to him,
　As he sang upon a tree!

James Stephens

SILVER

Slowly, silently, now the moon
Walks the night in her silver shoon;
This way, and that, she peers, and sees
Silver fruit upon silver trees;
One by one the casements catch
Her beams beneath the silvery thatch;
Couched in his kennel, like a log,
With paws of silver sleeps the dog;
From their shadowy cote the white breasts peep
Of doves in a silver-feathered sleep;
A harvest mouse goes scampering by,
With silver claws, and silver eye;
And moveless fish in the water gleam,
By silver reeds in a silver stream.

Walter de la Mare

FROLIC

The children were shouting together
    And racing along the sands,
A glimmer of dancing shadows,
    A dove-like flutter of hands.

The stars were shouting in heaven,
    The sun was chasing the moon,
The game was the same as the children's,
    They danced to the self-same tune.

The whole of the world was merry,
    One joy from the vale to the height,
Where the blue woods of twilight encircled
    The lovely lawns of the light.

A.E.

THE TREE IN THE GARDEN

There's a tree out in our garden which is very nice to climb,
And I often go and climb it when it's fine in summer time,
And when I've climbed right up it I pretend it's not a tree
But a ship in which I'm sailing, far away across the sea.

Its branches are the rigging and the grass so far below
I make believe's the ocean over which my ship must go;
And when the wind is blowing then I really seem to be
A-sailing, sailing, sailing, far away across the sea.

Then I hunt for desert islands and I very often find
A chest stuffed full of treasure which some pirate's left behind —
My good ship's hold is filled with gold – it all belongs to me —
For I've found it when I'm sailing far away across the sea.

It's a lovely game to play at – though the tree trunk's rather green,
Still, when I'm in my bath at night I always come quite clean.
And so through all the summer, in my good ship Treasure-Tree,
I shall often go a-sailing far away across the sea.

Christine Chaundler

THE BOY'S SONG

Where the pools are bright and deep,
Where the grey trout lies asleep,
Up the river and o'er the lea —
That's the way for Billy and me.

Where the blackbird sings the latest,
Where the hawthorn blooms the sweetest,
Where the nestlings chirp and flee —
That's the way for Billy and me.

Where the mowers mow the cleanest,
Where the hay lies thick and greenest,
There to trace the homeward bee —
That's the way for Billy and me.

Where the hazel bank is steepest,
Where the shadow falls the deepest,
Where the clustering nuts fall free —
That's the way for Billy and me.

There let us walk, there let us play,
Through the meadows, among the hay,
Up the water, and o'er the lea —
That's the way for Billy and me.

James Hogg

JOYS

We may shut our eyes,
But we cannot help knowing
That skies are clear
And grass is growing;
The breeze comes whispering in our ear,
That dandelions are blossoming near,
That corn has sprouted,
That streams are flowing,
That the river is bluer than the sky,
That the robin is plastering his home hard by.

J. R. Lowell

THE LIGHTHOUSE

Burning upon some hidden shore
  Across the sea one night
('A little reef,' the Captain said),
  We saw a shining light.

He said there was a lighthouse there
  Where, lonely in the sea,
Men lived to guard that moving light,
  And trim the lamp for me.

For me, for him, for every ship
  That passes by that way.
I thought it must be strange and quiet
  To be there every day.

They have no shops, no fields, no streets;
  No whispering sound of trees,
But always shouting at their feet
  The great voice of the seas.

And when we sleep at night they wake,
  And over every wave
They send that straight strong arm of light
  Stretched like a rope to save.

Marjorie Wilson

THE SEA

Take your bucket, and take your spade,
  And come to the sea with me,
Building castles upon the sand
  Is the game for you and me!
Races run with the tumbling waves,
Then rest awhile in the cool, dark caves.
Oh, the greatest joy in the summer time
  Is the sea, the sparkling sea!

E. M. Adams

RAINY NIGHTS

I like the town on rainy nights
　　When everything is wet —
When all the town has magic lights
　　And streets of shining jet!

When all the rain about the town
　　Is like a looking-glass,
And all the lights are upside-down
　　Below me as I pass.

In all the pools are velvet skies,
　　And down the dazzling street
A fairy city gleams and lies
　　In beauty at my feet.

Irene Thompson

THE AEROPLANE

Look at the aeroplane
　　Up in the sky,
Seems like a giant lark
　　Soaring on high.

See! on its outspread wing
　　Flashes the light;
There sits the pilot brave
　　Guiding its flight.

Hark! what a whirring song
　　Comes from its throat,
Purr, purr of the engine,
　　Its only note.

Now! high and higher yet,
　　Upward it goes,
Till but a tiny speck
　　'Gainst heaven it shows.

Oh! here it is again,
　　Big as before,
Gracefully gliding down
　　To earth once more.

Jeannie Kirby

CASTLES IN THE SAND

I've built a castle in the sand
　　In less than half an hour,
With grim portcullis, and a moat,
　　And battlements and tower.

The seaweed banners wave, and when
　　I let the drawbridge down,
The knights come riding two by two
　　In armour rusty brown.

And ladies lean from turrets high,
　　And watch them as they pass,
And wave their floating silken scarves,
　　As light and green as grass.

But see! across the shining sand,
　　That enemy the sea
Creeps slowly to my castle walls,
　　Advancing stealthily.

No bugles sound a wild alarm,
　　No warders close the gate;
The knights and ladies disappear,
　　And all alone I wait.

For where my fairy fortress stood
　　And glistened in the sun,
There lies a heap of ruins now,
　　My work is all undone.

Dorothy Baker

FLYING

I saw the moon,
One windy night,
Flying so fast —
All silvery white —
Over the sky
Like a toy balloon
Loose from its string —
A runaway moon.
The frosty stars
Went racing past,
Chasing her on
Ever so fast.
Then everyone said,
'It's the clouds that fly,
And the stars and moon
Stand still in the sky.'
But I don't mind —
I saw the moon
Sailing away
Like a toy
Balloon.

J. M. Westrup

SWINGING

Slowly, slowly, swinging low,
Let me see how far I go!
Slowly, slowly, keeping low,
I see where the wild flowers grow!

(*Getting quicker*) :

Quicker, quicker,
Swinging higher,
I can see
A shining spire!
Quicker, quicker,
Swinging higher,
I can see
The sunset's fire!

Faster, faster,
Through the air,
I see almost
Everywhere.
Woods and hills,
And sheep that stare —
And things I never
Knew were there!

(Getting slower):
Slower, slower, now I go,
Swinging, dreaming, getting low;
Slowly, slowly, down I go —
Till I touch the grass below.

Irene Thompson

GLOW-WORMS

With a yellow lantern
  I take the road at night,
And chase the flying shadows
  By its cheerful light.

From the banks and hedgerows
  Other lanterns shine,
Tiny elfin glimmers,
  Not so bright as mine.

Those are glow-worm lanterns,
  Coloured green and blue,
Orange, red and purple,
  Gaily winking through.

See the glow-worms hurry!
  See them climb and crawl!
They go to light the dancers
  At the fairy ball.

P. A. Ropes

SHERWOOD

Sherwood in the twilight, is Robin Hood awake?
Grey and ghostly shadows are gliding through the brake;
Shadows of the dappled deer, dreaming of the morn,
Dreaming of a shadowy man that winds a shadowy horn.

Robin Hood is here again; all his merry thieves
Hear a ghostly bugle-note, shivering through the leaves,
Calling as he used to call, faint and far away,
In Sherwood, in Sherwood, about the break of day.

Merry, merry England has kissed the lips of June;
All the wings of fairyland are here beneath the moon;
Like a flight of rose-leaves fluttering in a mist
Of opal and ruby and pearl and amethyst.

Merry, merry England is waking as of old,
With eyes of blither hazel and hair of brighter gold:
For Robin Hood is here again beneath the bursting spray
In Sherwood, in Sherwood, about the break of day.

Love is in the greenwood building him a house
Of wild rose and hawthorn and honeysuckle boughs;
Love is in the greenwood: dawn is in the skies;
And Marian is waiting with a glory in her eyes.

Hark! the dazzled laverock climbs the golden steep:
Marian is waiting: is Robin Hood asleep?
Round the fairy grass-rings frolic elf and fay,
In Sherwood, in Sherwood, about the break of day.

Oberon, Oberon, rake away the gold,
Rake away the red leaves, roll away the mould,
Rake away the gold leaves, roll away the red,
And wake Will Scarlett from his leafy forest bed.

Friar Tuck and Little John are riding down together
With quarter-staff and drinking-can and grey goose-feather;
The dead are coming back again; the years are rolled away
In Sherwood, in Sherwood, about the break of day.

Softly over Sherwood the South wind blows;
All the heart of England hid in every rose
Hears across the greenwood the sunny whisper leap,
Sherwood in the red dawn, is Robin Hood asleep?

Hark, the voice of England wakes him as of old
And, shattering the silence with a cry of brighter gold,
Bugles in the greenwood echo from the steep,
Sherwood in the red dawn, is Robin Hood asleep?

Where the deer are gliding down the shadowy glen
All across the glades of fern he calls his merry men;
Doublets of the Lincoln green glancing through the May
In Sherwood, in Sherwood, about the break of day;

Call them and they answer; from aisles of oak and ash
Rings the *Follow! Follow!* and the boughs begin to crash;
The ferns begin to flutter and the flowers begin to fly;
And through the crimson dawning the robber band goes by.

Robin! Robin! Robin! all his merry thieves
Answer as the bugle-note shivers through the leaves;
Calling as he used to call, faint and far away,
In Sherwood, in Sherwood, about the break of day.

A. Noyes

COBWEBS

Between me and the rising sun,
This way and that the cobwebs run;
Their myriad wavering lines of light
Dance up the hill and out of sight.

There is no land possesses half
So many lines of telegraph
As those the spider-elves have spun
Between me and the rising sun.

E. L. M. King

125

THE WINDMILL

If you should bid me make a choice
    'Twixt wind- and water-mill,
In spite of all the mill-pond's charms
I'd take those gleaming, sweeping arms
    High on a windy hill.

The miller stands before his door
    And whistles for a breeze;
And, when it comes, his sails go round
With such a mighty rushing sound
    You think of heavy seas.

And if the wind declines to blow
    The miller takes a nap
(Although he'd better spend an hour
In brushing at the dust and flour
    That line his coat and cap.)

Now, if a water-mill were his,
    Such rest he'd never know,
For round and round his crashing wheel,
His dashing, splashing, plashing wheel,
    Unceasingly would go.

So, if you'd bid me take a choice
    'Twixt wind- and water-mill,
In spite of all a mill-pond's charms,
I'd take those gleaming, sweeping arms
    High on a windy hill.

E. V. Lucas

PIPPA'S SONG

The year's at the spring;
The day's at the morn;
Morning's at seven;
The hill-side's dew-pearled;
The lark's on the wing;
The snail's on the thorn;
God's in His heaven —
All's right with the world!

Robert Browning

THE LIGHTS

I know the ships that pass by day:
I guess their business, grave or gay,
  And spy their flags, and learn their names,
    And whence they come and where they go —
    But in the night I only know
  Some little starry flames.

And yet I think these jewelled lights
Have meanings full as noonday sights:
  For every emerald signs to me
    That ship and souls are harbour near,
    And every ruby rich and clear
  Proclaims them bound for sea.

And all the yellow diamonds set
On mast and deck and hull in jet
  Have meanings real as day can show:
    They tell of care, of watchful eyes,
    Of labour, slumber, hopes, and sighs —
  Of human joy and woe.

O ships that come and go by night,
God's blessing be on every light!

J. J. Bell

WHITE HORSES

Far out at sea
  There are horses to ride,
Little white horses
  That race with the tide.

Their tossing manes
  Are the white sea-foam,
And the lashing winds
  Are driving them home —

To shadowy stables
  Fast they must flee,
To the great green caverns
  Down under the sea.

Irene F. Pawsey

WIND AND THE LEAVES

'Come, little Leaves,' said the Wind one day,
'Come o'er the meadows with me, and play;
Put on your dresses of red and gold;
Summer is gone, and the days grow cold.'

Soon as the Leaves heard the Wind's loud call,
Down they came fluttering, one and all;
Over the fields they danced and flew,
Singing the soft little songs they knew.

Dancing and whirling the little Leaves went;
Winter had called them, and they were content.
Soon, fast asleep in their earthy beds,
The snow laid a coverlet over their heads.

WHERE LIES THE LAND

Where lies the land to which the ship would go?
Far, far ahead is all her seamen know.
And where the land she travels from? Away,
Far, far behind, is all that they can say.

On sunny noons upon the deck's smooth face,
Linked arm in arm, how pleasant here to pace!
Or, o'er the stern reclining, watch below
The foaming wake far-widening as we go.

On stormy nights when wild north-westerns rave,
How proud a thing to fight with wind and wave!
The dripping sailor on the reeling mast
Exults to bear, and scorns to wish it past.

Where lies the land to which the ship would go?
Far, far ahead is all her seamen know.
And where the land she travels from? Away,
Far, far behind is all that they can say.

Arthur Hugh Clough

All Creatures Great and Small

PART FIVE

Little children, never give
Pain to things that feel and live

DUCK'S DITTY

All along the backwater,
    Through the rushes tall,
Ducks are a-dabbling,
    Up tails all!

Ducks' tails, drakes' tails,
    Yellow feet a-quiver,
Yellow bills all out of sight
    Busy in the river!

Slushy green undergrowth
    Where the roach swim,
Here we keep our larder
    Cool and full and dim!

Every one for what he likes!
    We like to be
Heads down, tails up,
    Dabbling free!

High in the blue above
    Swifts whirl and call —
We are down a-dabbling,
    Up tails all!

Kenneth Grahame

THE TADPOLE

Underneath the water-weeds
    Small and black, I wriggle,
And life is most surprising!
    Wiggle! waggle! wiggle!
There's every now and then a most
    Exciting change in me,
I wonder, wiggle! waggle!
    What I *shall* turn out to be!

E. E. Gould

THE EAGLE

He clasps the crag with crooked hands;
Close to the sun in lonely lands,
Ringed with the azure world, he stands.

The wrinkled sea beneath him crawls;
He watches from his mountain walls,
And like a thunderbolt he falls.

Lord Tennyson

GAY ROBIN IS SEEN NO MORE

Gay Robin is seen no more:
    He is gone with the snow.
    For winter is o'er
    And Robin will go.
In need he was fed, and now he is fled
    Away to his secret nest.
    No more will he stand
    Begging for crumbs,
    No longer he comes
    Beseeching our hand
    And showing his breast
    At window and door:
Gay Robin is seen no more.

Blithe Robin is heard no more:
    He gave us his song
    When summer was o'er
    And winter was long:
He sang for his bread, and now he is fled
    Away to his secret nest,
    And there in the green
    Early and late
    Alone to his mate
    He pipeth unseen
    And swelleth his breast;
    For us it is o'er:
Blithe Robin is heard no more.

Robert Bridges

THE BROWN THRUSH

There's a merry brown thrush sitting up in the tree,
'He's singing to me! He's singing to me!'
And what does he say, little girl, little boy?
'Oh, the world's running over with joy!
Don't you hear? don't you see?
Hush! Look! In my tree
I'm as happy as happy can be!'

And the brown thrush keeps singing, 'A nest do you see,
And five eggs, hid by me in the juniper-tree?
Don't meddle! don't touch! little girl, little boy,
Or the world will lose some of its joy!
Now I'm glad! now I'm free!
And I always shall be,
If you never bring sorrow to me.'

So the merry brown thrush sings away in the tree,
To you and to me, to you and to me;
And he sings all the day, little girl, little boy,
'Oh, the world's running over with joy!
But long it won't be,
Don't you know? don't you see?
Unless we are as good as can be!'

Lucy Larcom

THE CURLIEST THING

The squirrel is the curliest thing
    I think I ever saw;
He curls his back, he curls his tail,
    He curls each little paw,
He curls his little vest so white,
    His little coat so grey —
He is the most curled-up wee soul
    Out in the woods at play!

THE BIRDS ON THE SCHOOL WINDOWSILL

Robin :   I'm hungry, oh so hungry!
            I'd love a piece of bread!

Sparrow : I've looked for nice cold water,
            But found hard ice instead.

Birds :   Please, please, do give us food and drink!
            You boys and girls are kind, I think.

Alec :   Here's a piece of crust.

Betty :   Here's another too.

Charles : Don't be frightened, pretty birds,
            We love you, yes, we do.

Dorothy : Here's a drink of water
            In a little dish:
            Help yourselves, poor thirsty birds;
            There's still more if you wish.

Children : Come again, Cock Sparrow;
            Robin Redbreast, too,
            Please come every morning —
            There's always food for you.

Birds :   Thank you, thank you, children,
            And now we'll fly away
            To bring our hungry friends to share
            The feast we've found today.

Evelyn Dainty

PRAYER FOR GENTLENESS TO ALL CREATURES

To all the humble beasts there be,
To all the birds on land and sea,
Great Spirit, sweet protection give
That free and happy they may live!

And to our hearts the rapture bring
Of love for every living thing;
Make us all one kin, and bless
Our ways with Christ's own gentleness!

John Galsworthy

133

THE POOR SNAIL

The snail says, 'Alas!'
And the snail says, 'Alack!
Why must I carry
My house on my back?
You have a home
To go in and out,
Why must mine always be
Carried about?
Not any tables,
Not any chairs,
Not any windows,
Not any stairs,
Pity my misery,
Pity my wail —
For I must always be
Just a poor snail.'
But he's terribly slow,
So perhaps it's as well
That his shell is his home,
And his home is his shell.

J. M. Westrup

THE FIFTEEN ACRES

I cling and swing
On a branch, or sing
Through the cool, clear hush of Morning, O!
Or fling my wing
On the air, and bring
To sleepier birds a warning, O!
That the night's in flight,
And the sun's in sight,
And the dew is the grass adorning, O!
And the green leaves swing
As I sing, sing, sing.
Up by the river,
Down the dell,
To the little wee nest,
Where the big tree fell,
So early in the morning, O!

I flit and twit
In the sun for a bit
When his light so bright is shining, O!
Or sit and fit
My plumes, or knit
Straw plaits for the nest's nice lining, O!
And she with glee
Shows unto me
Underneath her wings reclining, O!
And I sing that Peg
Has an egg, egg, egg,
Up by the oat-field
Round the mill,
Past the meadow,
Down by the hill,
So early in the morning, O!

I stoop and swoop
On the air, or loop
Through the trees, and then go soaring, O!
To group with a troop
On the gusty poop
While the wind behind is roaring, O!
I skim and swim
By a cloud's red rim
And up to the azure flooring, O!
And my wide wings drip
As I slip, slip, slip
Down through the rain-drops,
Back where Peg
Broods in the nest
On the little white egg,
So early in the morning, O!

James Stephens

THE ELEPHANT

When people call this beast to mind,
They marvel more and more
At such a little tail behind
So LARGE a trunk before.

Hilaire Belloc

MICHAEL MET A WHITE DUCK

Michael met a white duck
  Walking on the green.
'How are you?' said Michael.
  'How fine the weather's been!
Blue sky and sunshine,
  All thro'out the day;
Not a single raindrop
  Came to spoil our play.'

But the sad white duck said,
  'I myself want rain.
I'd like to see the brooklets
  And the streams fill up again.
Now I can't go swimming,
  It really makes me cry
To see the little duckponds
  Look so very dry.'

But behold next morning,
  The clouds are looking black:
Down the rain came pouncing,
  Said the duck, 'Quack, quack.
Ponds are full of water,
  Ducks are full of joy.'
But someone else is not pleased,
  And that's the little boy.

J. Dupuy

ZOO MANNERS

Be careful what
  You say or do
When you visit the animals
  At the Zoo.

Don't make fun
  Of the Camel's hump —
He's very proud
  Of his noble bump.

Don't laugh too much
    At the Chimpanzee —
He thinks he's as wise
    As you or me.

And the Penguins
    Strutting round the lake
Can understand
    Remarks you make.

Treat them as well
    As they do you,
And you'll always be welcome
    At the Zoo.

Eileen Mathias

THE AUTUMN ROBIN

Sweet little bird in russet coat,
    The livery of the closing year,
I love thy lonely plaintive note
    And tiny whispering song to hear,
While on the stile or garden seat
    I sit to watch the falling leaves,
The song thy little joys repeat
    My loneliness relieves.

John Clare

THE BROWN FROG

Today as I went out to play
I saw a brown frog in the way,
I know that frogs are smooth and green,
But this was brown – what could it mean?
I asked a lady in the road ;
She said it was a spotted toad!

Mary K. Robinson

MILK FOR THE CAT

When the tea is brought at five o'clock,
   And all the neat curtains are drawn with care,
The little black cat with bright green eyes
   Is suddenly purring there.

At first she pretends, having nothing to do,
   She has come in merely to blink by the grate;
But, though tea may be late or the milk may be sour,
   She is never late.

And presently her agate eyes
   Take a soft large milky haze,
And her independent casual glance
   Becomes a stiff hard gaze.

Then she stamps her claws or lifts her ears,
   Or twists her tail and begins to stir,
Till suddenly all her lithe body becomes
   One breathing trembling purr.

The children eat and wriggle and laugh;
   The two old ladies stroke their silk:
But the cat is grown small and thin with desire,
   Transformed to a creeping lust for milk.

The white saucer like some full moon descends
   At last from the clouds of the table above;
She sighs and dreams and thrills and glows,
   Transfigured with love.

She nestles over the shining rim,
   Buries her chin in the creamy sea;
Her tail hangs loose; each drowsy paw
   Is doubled under each bending knee.

A long dim ecstasy holds her life;
   Her world is an infinite shapeless white,
Till her tongue has curled the last holy drop,
   Then she sinks back into the night.

Draws and dips her body to heap
   Her sleepy nerves in the great arm-chair,
Lies defeated and buried deep
   Three or four hours unconscious there.

Harold Monro

A FRIEND IN THE GARDEN

He is not John, the gardener,
   And yet the whole day long
Employs himself most usefully,
   The flower-beds among.

He is not Tom, the pussy-cat,
   And yet the other day,
With stealthy stride and glistening eye,
   He crept upon his prey.

He is not Dash, the dear old dog,
   And yet, perhaps, if you
Took pains with him and petted him,
   You'd come to love him too.

He's not a Blackbird, though he chirps
   And though he once was black;
And now he wears a loose grey coat,
   All wrinkled on the back.

He's got a very dirty face,
   And very shining eyes!
He sometimes comes and sits indoors;
   He looks – and p'r'aps is – wise.

But in a sunny flower-bed
   He has his fixed abode;
He eats the things that eat my plants —
   He is a friendly *Toad*.

Juliana Horatia Ewing

THE FIELD-MOUSE

I live among the grasses,
  And watch them growing high,
And as the summer passes
  They seem to touch the sky.

The Spiders are my neighbours,
  Busy people they,
I watch them at their labours,
  Spinning day by day.

The Earwig comes a-calling,
  The Ladybird as well,
And Snails go slowly crawling,
  And Slugs, without a shell.

The Bumble, fat and furry,
  A flying visit pays,
And Caterpillars hurry
  Adown the grassy ways.

I am your little brother,
  A Mouse in brown and grey,
So if we meet each other,
  Please let me run away!

Enid Blyton

THE ELEPHANT

Here comes the elephant
  Swaying along
With his cargo of children
  All singing a song:
To the tinkle of laughter
  He goes on his way,
And his cargo of children
  Have crowned him with May.
His legs are in leather
  And padded his toes;

He can root up an oak
　　With a whisk of his nose:
With a wave of his trunk
　　And a turn of his chin
He can pull down a house,
　　Or pick up a pin.
Beneath his grey forehead
　　A little eye peers!
Of what is he thinking
　　Between those wide ears?
Of what does he think?
　　If he wished to tease,
He could twirl his keeper
　　Over the trees:
If he were not kind,
　　He could play cup and ball
With Robert and Helen
　　And Uncle Paul:
But that grey forehead,
　　Those crinkled ears,
Have learned to be kind
　　In a hundred years!
And so with the children
　　He goes on his way
To the tinkle of laughter
　　And crowned with the May.

Herbert Asquith

THE CATERPILLAR

Brown and furry
Caterpillar in a hurry,
Take your walk
To the shady leaf, or stalk,
Or what not,
Which may be the chosen spot.
No toad spy you,
Hovering bird of prey pass by you;
Spin and die,
To live again a butterfly.

Christina Rossetti

BROWNY BEE

Little Mr Browny Bee,
Gather honey for my tea;
Come into my garden, do,
I've every kind of flower for you.

There's blossom on my tiny tree,
And daisies in the grass you'll see;
There's lavender, and scented stocks.
And rows of frilly hollyhocks.

I've marigolds, and pansies too,
And Canterbury-bells of blue;
There's rosemary, and scented thyme,
And foxglove heads you'll love to climb.

I've gilly-flowers, and roses red,
All waiting in my garden bed;
Seek honey where my flowers are
To fill my little honey-jar.

Irene F. Pawsey

THE RABBIT

Brown bunny sits inside his burrow
    Till everything is still,
Then out he slips along the furrow,
    Or up the grassy hill.

He nibbles all about the bushes
    Or sits to wash his face,
But at a sound he stamps, and rushes
    At a surprising pace.

You see some little streaks and flashes,
    A last sharp twink of white,
As down his hidey-hole he dashes
    And disappears from sight.

Edith King

WHAT THE THRUSH SAYS

'Come and see! Come and see!'
The thrush pipes out of the hawthorn tree:
And I and Dicky on tiptoe go
To see what treasures he wants to show
His call is clear as a call can be —
And 'Come and see!' he says:
　　　　'Come and see!'

'Come and see! Come and see!'
His house is there in the hawthorn-tree:
The neatest house that ever you saw,
Built all of mosses and twigs and straw:
The folk who built were his wife and he —
And 'Come and see!' he says:
　　　　'Come and see!'

'Come and see! Come and See!'
Within this house there are treasures three:
So warm and snug in its curve they lie —
Like three bright bits out of Spring's blue sky.
We would not hurt them, he knows: not we!
So 'Come and see!' he says:
　　　　'Come and see!'

Queenie Scott-Hopper

ONE BLACKBIRD

The stars must make an awful noise
　　In whirling round the sky;
Yet somehow I can't even hear
　　Their loudest song or sigh.

So it is wonderful to think
　　One blackbird can outsing
The voice of all the swarming stars
　　On any day in spring.

Harold Monro

BIRDS' NESTS

'Caw,' said the rook,
'My nest is here. Look!
At the top of a tree
Is the best place for me.'

'Coo,' called the dove
From her nest above;
'In the fork of a beech
I am quite out of reach.'

'Hark!' carolled a lark,
'I sing until dark,
My nest on the ground
Is not easily found.'

'Hush!' sang a thrush,
'In this holly bush
I am safe from all harm
With my blue eggs so warm.'

But Robin Redbreast
From her mossy nest
Said never a word,
What a wise little bird!

Millicent Seager

THE CROW

Old Crow, upon the tall tree-top
 I see you sitting at your ease,
You hang upon the highest bough
 And balance in the breeze.

How many miles you've been today
 Upon your wing so strong and black,
And steered across the dark grey sky
 Without a guide or track;

Above the city wrapped in smoke,
    Green fields and rivers flowing clear;
Now tell me, as you passed them o'er,
    What did you see and hear?

The old crow shakes his sooty wing
    And answers hoarsely, 'Caw, caw, caw,'
And that is all the crow can tell
    Of what he heard and saw.

Mrs Alexander

TO A CRICKET

Voice of summer, keen and shrill,
Chirping round the winter fire,
Of thy song I never tire,
Weary others as they will,
For thy song with summer's filled —
Filled with sunshine, filled with June;
Firelight echo of that noon
Heard in fields when all is still
In the golden light of May,
Bringing scents of new-mown hay,
Bees, and birds, and flowers away,
Prithee, haunt my fireside still,
Voice of summer, keen and shrill.

William Cox Bennett

THE BIRD BATH

There is a bird bath on our grass,
I wait to watch it as I pass,
And see the little sparrow things
Stand on the edge with flapping wings
They give each eye a merry wink
And stoop to take a little drink,
And then, before I'm fairly gone,
They bath with all their clothing on!

Florence Hoatson

THE CITY MOUSE AND THE GARDEN MOUSE

The city mouse lives in a house;
　　The garden mouse lives in a bower,
He's friendly with the frogs and toads,
　　And sees the pretty plants in flower.

The city mouse eats bread and cheese;
　　The garden mouse eats what he can;
We will not grudge him seeds and stocks,
　　Poor little timid furry man.

Christina Rossetti

NICHOLAS NYE

Thistle and darnel and·dock grew there,
　　And a bush, in the corner, of may,
On the orchard wall I used to sprawl
　　In the blazing heat of the day;
Half asleep and half awake
　　While the birds went twittering by,
And nobody there my lone to share
　　But Nicholas Nye.

Nicholas Nye was lean and grey,
　　Lame of leg and old,
More than a score of donkey's years
　　He had seen since he was foaled;
He munched the thistles, purple and spiked,
　　Would sometimes stoop and sigh,
And turn to his head, as if he said,
　　'Poor Nicholas Nye!'

Alone with his shadow he'd drowse in the meadow
　　Lazily swinging his tail,
At break of day he used to bray —
　　Not much too hearty and hale;
But a wonderful gumption was under his skin,
　　And a clean calm light in his eye,
And once in a while, he'd smile —
　　Would Nicholas Nye.

Seem to be smiling at me, he would,
   From his bush, in the corner, of may —
Bony and ownerless, widowed and worn,
   Knobble-kneed, lonely and grey
   And over the grass would seem to pass
   'Neath the deep dark blue of the sky,
Something much better than words between me
   And Nicholas Nye.

But dusk would come in the apple boughs,
   The green of the glow-worm shine,
The birds in nest would crouch to rest,
   And home I'd trudge to mine;
And there, in the moonlight, dark with dew,
   Asking no wherefore nor why,
Would brood like a ghost, and as still as a post,
   Old Nicholas Nye.

                              Walter de la Mare

ROBIN'S SONG

Robins sang in England,
   Frost or rain or snow,
All the long December days
   Endless years ago.

Robins sang in England
   Before the Legions came,
Before our English fields were tilled
   Or England was a name.

Robins sang in England
   When forests dark and wild
Stretched across from sea to sea
   And Jesus was a child.

Listen! in the frosty dawn
   From his leafless bough
The same brave song he ever sang
   A robin's singing now.

                              Rodney Bennett

GRASSHOPPER GREEN

Grasshopper Green is a comical chap;
    He lives on the best of fare.
Bright little trousers, jacket and cap,
    These are his summer wear.
Out in the meadow he loves to go,
    Playing away in the sun;
It's hopperty, skipperty, high and low —
    Summer's the time for fun.

Grasshopper Green has a quaint little house
    It's under the hedgerow gay.
Grandmother Spider, as still as a mouse,
    Watches him over the way.
Gladly he's calling the children, I know,
    Out in the beautiful sun;
It's hopperty, skipperty, high and low —
    Summer's the time for fun.

THE PIG'S TAIL

A furry coat has the bear to wear,
    The tortoise a coat of mail,
The yak has more than his share of hair,
    But – the pig has the curly tail.

The elephant's tusks are sold for gold,
    The slug leaves a silver trail,
The parrot is never too old to scold,
    But – the pig has the curly tail.

The lion can either roar or snore,
    The cow gives milk in a pail,
The dog can guard a door, and more,
    But – the pig has the curly tail.

The monkey makes you smile a while,
    The tiger makes you quail,
The fox has many a wile of guile,
    But – the pig has the curly tail.

For the rest of the beasts that prey or play,
   From tiny mouse to the whale,
There's much that I could say today,
   But – the pig has the curly tail.

Norman Ault

THE SNAIL

To grass, or leaf, or fruit, or wall,
The Snail sticks close, nor fears to fall,
As if he grew there, house and all
                  Together.

Within that house secure he hides,
When danger imminent betides
Of storms, or other harm besides,
                  Of weather.

Give but his horns the slightest touch.
His self-collecting power is such,
He shrinks into his house with much
                  Displeasure.

Where'er he dwells, he dwells alone,
Except himself has chattels none,
Well satisfied to be his own
                  Whole treasure.

Thus hermit-like, his life he leads,
Nor partner of his Banquet needs,
And if he meets one, only feeds
                  The faster.

Who seeks him must be worse than blind
(He and his house are so combined)
If, finding it, he fails to find
                  Its master.

William Cowper

GREY BROTHER

The grey goat grazed on the hill
   The grey hare grazed by his side,
And never a word they said
   From morning till eventide,
And never a word they said,
   Though each understood the other,
For the wind that played on the hill
   Whispered, 'My dear grey brother.'

The grey goat went home at dusk,
   Down to the cottage door,
The grey hare scuttled away
   To his burrow across the moor.
And never a word they said,
   Though each understood the other,
For the wind that slept on the hill
   Murmured, 'Good night, grey brother.'

U. M. Montgomery

THE GREEDY LITTLE PIG

A little pig lived in a sty,
   He fed on meals three times a day,
He drank sweet milk from a shining trough
   And slept at night on a bed of hay.

This little pig once left his sty,
   And roamed three fields or more away,
He found the slope where the oak trees grew
   And where the plump brown acorns lay.
     And he ate, and he ate,
      As little pigs do;
     He ate and he ate,
      The whole day through.
   Then he came back home to his bed of hay,
   Grunt-grunt-grunting all the way.

Irene F. Pawsey

MR SQUIRREL

I saw a brown squirrel today in the wood,
He ran here and there just as fast as he could;
I think he was looking for nuts for his store,
He'd found quite a lot, but he still wanted more.

He can't find much food once the winter is here,
He hides all his nuts in a hole somewhere near,
Then settles himself for a long winter sleep,
Coming out now and then for a nut and a peep.

His long bushy tail keeps him cosy and warm,
His nest's far away from the wind and the storm
But when springtime comes back, I think that, maybe,
He'll be waiting again in the woodland for me.

V. M. Julian

THE COW AND THE ASS

Beside a green meadow a stream used to flow,
So clear, you might see the white pebbles below;
To this cooling brook, the warm cattle would stray.
To stand in the shade on a hot summer's day.

A cow quite oppressed by the heat of the sun,
Came here to refresh as she often had done;
And, standing quite still, stooping over the stream
Was musing, perhaps – or perhaps she might dream.

But soon a brown ass of respectable look
Came trotting up also to taste of the brook,
And to nibble a few of the daisies and grass.
'How d'ye do?' said the cow. 'How d'ye do?' said the ass.

'Take a seat!' said the cow, gently waving her hand.
'By no means, dear madam,' said he, 'while you stand!'
Then, stooping to drink, with a very low bow,
'Ma'am, your health!' said the ass.
'Thank you, sir,' said the cow.

Ann and Jane Taylor

WHALE

Wouldn't you like to be a whale
And sail serenely by —
An eighty-foot whale from the tip of your tail
And a tiny briny eye?
Wouldn't you like to wallow
Where nobody says 'Come out!'?
Wouldn't you *love* to swallow
And blow all the brine about?
Wouldn't you like to be always clean
But never to have to wash, I mean,
And wouldn't you love to spout —
   O yes, just think —
A feather of spray as you sail away,
And rise and sink and rise and sink,
And blow all the brine about?

Geoffrey Dearmer

FAN, THE FILLY

   Bumpety, bumpety, bump.
    The horses run down the green hill.
There's Fan the wild filly again at her tricks!
She rears at the fence and she knocks down the sticks
To get at the hay at the base of the ricks.
   Bumpety, bumpety, bump.

   Bumpety, bumpety, bump.
    The horses run down the green hill.
They're all of them wanting a share of the hay
The Roan and the Dapple, the Black and the Bay;
They follow the filly and gallop away
   Bumpety, bumpety, bump.

   Bumpety, bumpety, bump.
    The horses run up the green hill.
For old Farmer Brown has come out with his man
To halter the mischievous filly called Fan,
And sell her for gold at the Fair if he can.
   Bumpety, bumpety, bump.

Bumpety, bumpety, bump.
       The horses run up the green hill,
But where there were five there are now only four,
For Fan the wild filly will gallop no more;
She stands in the shafts at a gentleman's door.
       Bumpety, bumpety, bump.

Wilfred Thorley

THE TYGER

Tyger! Tyger! burning bright
In the forests of the night,
What immortal hand or eye
Could frame thy fearful symmetry?

In what distant deeps or skies
Burnt the fire of thine eyes?
On what wings dare he aspire?
What the hand dare seize the fire?

And what shoulder, and what art,
Could twist the sinews of thy heart?
And when thy heart began to beat,
What dread hand? and what dread feet?

What the hammer? what the chain?
In what furnace was thy brain?
What the anvil? what dread grasp
Dare its deadly terrors clasp?

When the stars threw down their spears,
And watered Heaven with their tears,
Did he smile his work to see?
Did He who made the Lamb make thee?

Tyger! Tyger! burning bright
In the forests of the night,
What immortal hand or eye,
Dare frame thy fearful symmetry?

William Blake

THE OLD BROWN HORSE

The old brown horse looks over the fence
  In a weary sort of way;
He seems to be saying to all who pass:
  'Well, folks, I've had my day —
I'm simply watching the world go by,
  And nobody seems to mind,
As they're dashing past in their motor-cars,
  A horse who is lame and half-blind.'

The old brown horse has a shaggy coat,
  But once he was young and trim,
And he used to trot through the woods and lanes
  With the man who was fond of him.
But his master rides in a motor-car,
  And it makes him feel quite sad
When he thinks of the days that used to be,
  And of all the times they had.

Sometimes a friendly soul will stop
  Near the fence, where the tired old head
Rests wearily on the topmost bar,
  And a friendly word is said.
Then the old brown horse gives a little sigh
  As he feels the kindly touch
Of a hand on his mane or his shaggy coat,
  And he doesn't mind so much.

So if you pass by the field one day,
  Just stop for a word or two
With the old brown horse who was once as young
  And as full of life as you.
He'll love the touch of your soft young hand,
  And I know he'll seem to say —
'Oh, thank you, friend, for the kindly thought
  For a horse who has had his day.'

W. F. Holmes

THE NIGHTINGALE

The speckled bird sings in the tree
   When all the stars are silver-pale.
Come, children, walk the night with me,
   And we shall hear the nightingale.

The nightingale is a shy bird,
   He flits before you through the night.
And now the sleepy vale is stirred
   Through all its green and gold and white.

The moon leans from her place to hear,
   The stars shed golden star-dust down,
For now comes in the sweet o' the year,
   The country's gotten the greenest gown.

The blackbird turns upon his bed,
   The thrush has oped a sleeping eye,
Quiet each downy sleepy-head;
   But who goes singing up the sky?

It is, it is the nightingale,
   In the tall tree upon the hill.
To moonlight and the dewy vale
   The nightingale will sing his fill.

He's but a homely, speckled bird,
   But he has gotten a golden flute,
And when his wondrous song is heard
   Blackbird and thrush and lark are mute.

Troop, children dear, out to the night,
   Clad in the moonlight silver-pale,
And in the world of green and white
   'Tis you shall hear the nightingale.

Katharine Tynan

THE HEDGEHOG AND HIS COAT

The owls have feathers lined with down
   To keep them nice and warm;
The rats have top-coats soft and brown
   To wrap in from the storm;
And nearly every bird and beast
   Has cosy suits to wear,
But Mr Hedgehog has the least
   Of any for his share.

His back is stuck with prickly pins
   That breezes whistle through,
And when the winter-time begins
   The only thing to do
Is just to find a leafy spot,
   And curl up from the rain,
Until the Spring comes, bright and hot,
   To waken him again.

The owls and rats and all their folk
   Are soft and smooth to touch,
But hedgehogs are not nice to stroke,
   Their prickles hurt so much.
So, though it looks a little queer,
His coat is best of all;
For nobody could interfere
   With such a bristly ball!

Elizabeth Fleming

TO THE CUCKOO

O blithe new-comer, I have heard,
   I hear thee, and rejoice:
O Cuckoo! shall I call thee bird
   Or but a wandering voice?

While I am lying on the grass,
    Thy two-fold shout I hear;
From hill to hill it seems to pass,
    At once far off and near.

Though babbling only to the vale
    Of sunshine and of flowers,
Thou bringest unto me a tale
    Of visionary hours.

Thrice, welcome, darling of the Spring!
    Even yet thou art to me
No bird, but an invisible thing,
    A voice, a mystery.

W. Wordsworth

KINDNESS TO ANIMALS

Little children, never give
Pain to things that feel and live:
Let the gentle robin come
For the crumbs you save at home —
As his meat you throw along
He'll repay you with a song;
Never hurt the timid hare
Peeping from her green grass lair
Let her come and sport and play
On the lawn at close of day;
The little lark goes soaring high
To the bright windows of the sky,
Singing as if 'twere always spring,
And fluttering on an untired wing —
Oh! let him sing his happy song,
Nor do these gentle creatures wrong.

THE PLAINT OF THE CAMEL

Canary-birds feed on sugar and seed,
   Parrots have crackers to crunch;
And as for the poodles, they tell me the noodles
   Have chicken and cream for their lunch.
But there's never a question
About MY digestion,
   ANYTHING does for me.

Cats, you're aware, can repose in a chair,
   Chickens can roost upon rails;
Puppies are able to sleep in a stable,
   And oysters can slumber in pails.
But no one supposes
A poor Camel dozes.
   ANY PLACE does for me.

Lambs are enclosed where it's never exposed,
   Coops are constructed for hens;
Kittens are treated to houses well heated,
   And pigs are protected by pens.
But a Camel comes handy
Wherever it's sandy,
   ANYWHERE does for me,

People would laugh if you rode a giraffe,
   Or mounted the back of an ox;
It's nobody's habit to ride on a rabbit,
   Or try to bestraddle a fox.
But as for a Camel, he's
Ridden by families —
   ANY LOAD does for me.

A snake is as round as a hole in the ground;
   Weasels are wavy and sleek;
And no alligator could ever be straighter
   Than lizards that live in a creek.
But a camel's all lumpy,
And bumpy and humpy
   ANY SHAPE does for me.

Charles Edward Carryl

A Number of Things

PART SIX

I love all beauteous things
I seek and adore them

EVERYDAY THINGS

Millionaires, presidents – even kings
Can't get along without everyday things.

Were you president, king or millionaire,
You'd use a comb to comb your hair.

If you wished to be clean – and you would, I hope —
You'd take a bath with water and soap.

And you'd have to eat – if you wanted to eat —
Bread and vegetables, fish and meat;

While your drink for breakfast would probably be
Milk or chocolate, coffee or tea.

You'd have to wear – you could hardly refuse —
Under clothes, outer clothes, stockings and shoes.

If you wished to make a reminding note,
You'd take a pencil out of your coat;

And you couldn't sign a letter, I think,
With anything better than pen and ink.

If you wanted to read, you'd be sure to look
At newspaper, magazine, or book;

And if it happened that you were ill,
You'd down some oil or choke on a pill.

If you had a cold I can only suppose
You'd use a handkerchief for your nose.

When you wanted to rest your weary head,
Like other folks, you'd hop into bed.

Millionaries, presidents – even kings
Can't get along without everyday things.

Jean Ayer

THE WATCHMAKER'S SHOP

A street in our town
  Has a queer little shop
With tumble-down walls
  And a thatch on the top;
And all the wee windows
  With crookedy panes
Are shining and winking
  With watches and chains.

(All sorts and all sizes
  In silver and gold,
And brass ones and tin ones
  And new ones and old;
And clocks for the kitchen
  And clocks for the hall,
High ones and low ones
  And wag-at-the-wall.)

The watchmaker sits
  On a long-leggèd seat
And bids you the time
  Of the day when you meet;
And round and about him
  There's ticketty-tock
From the tiniest watch
  To the grandfather clock.

I wonder he doesn't
  Get tired of the chime
And all the clocks ticking
  And telling the time;
But there he goes winding
  Lest any should stop,
This queer little man
  In the watchmaker's shop.

Elizabeth Fleming

SNOW IN TOWN

Nothing is quite so quiet and clean
   As snow that falls in the night;
And isn't it jolly to jump from bed
   And find the whole world white?

It lies on the window ledges,
   It lies on the boughs of the trees,
While sparrows crowd at the kitchen door,
   With a pitiful 'If you please?'

It lies on the arm of the lamp-post,
   Where the lighter's ladder goes,
And the policeman under it beats his arms,
   And stamps to feel his toes;

No sound there is in the snowy road
   From the horse's cautious feet,
And all is hushed but the postman's knocks
   Rat-tatting down the street.

Till men come round with shovels
   To clear the snow away,
What a pity it is that when it falls
   They never let it stay!

Rickman Mark

MY PLAYMATE

I often wonder how it is
   That on a rainy day,
A little boy, just like myself,
   Comes out with me to play.

And we step in all the puddles
   When walking into town,
But though I stand the right way up,
   He's always upside-down.

I have to tread upon his feet,
    Which is a sorry sight,
With my right foot on his left foot,
    My left foot on his right.

I really wish he'd talk to me,
    He seems so very kind,
For when I look and smile at him
    He does the same, I find.

But I never hear him speaking,
    So surely he must be
In some strange land the other side,
    Just opposite to me.

Mary I. Osborn

IN DAYS GONE BY

I feel that in the days gone by
    I did not live with walls and roofs.
Long years ago in deserts dry
I lived beneath the open sky
    And heard the roar of thudding hoofs,
        And I was racing madly,
        My head bent to the wind,
        And fifty thousand horsemen
            Galloping behind!

I feel that in that long ago
    I must have been a Nomad child
Feeling the desert sun's fierce glow,
And then, in saddle, head bent low,
    Heading a horde of Bedouins wild.
        I shut my eyes an instant
        And see them in my mind,
        These fifty thousand horsemen
            Galloping, galloping,
        Fifty thousand horsemen
            Galloping behind!

Ida M. Mills

THE IDLERS

The gipsies lit their fires by the chalk-pit anew,
And the hoppled horses supped in the further dusk and dew;
The gnats flocked round the smoke like idlers as they were
And through the grass and bushes the owls began to churr.

An ell above the woods the last of sunset glowed
With a dusky gold that filled the pond beside the road;
The cricketers had done, the leas all silent lay,
And the carriers' clattering wheels went past and died away.

The gipsies lolled and gossipped, and ate their stolen swedes,
Made merry with mouth-organs, worked toys with piths of reeds:
The old wives puffed their pipes, nigh as black as their hair,
And not one of them all seemed to know the name of care.

Edmund Blunden

THE ENGINE DRIVER

Onward flies the rushing train,
Now in sunshine, now in rain;
Now through pleasant banks we ride,
Now o'er fenland stretching wide.

Now it is a forest nook,
Now a village by a brook,
Now a tunnel, black as night,
Shutting all things from the sight.

Now through meadows green we sweep,
Now below a wooded steep,
Now by smoky hives of men,
Now through quiet fields again.

Still the fiery steeds obey,
Still we rattle on our way;
Now beneath the placid moon,
Silvering the woods of June.

Now beneath a wilder sky,
Where the moon rides fast and high;
Now through snowflakes on the blast,
To the lights of home at last.

Who is he that drives the train,
In the sunshine and the rain;
Weather-beaten, bluff and strong,
Hero worthy of a song?

Who more earnest, brave and true,
In the work he has to do?
First in danger, first in blame,
No man earns a nobler name.

G.S.O.

THROUGH THE PORTHOLE
(*At Night*)

When I went to bed at night,
   Then my porthole was a frame:
If I watched a little while,
   I would find that pictures came.

Once I saw the mast-head light
   Of a far-off passing ship:
On the rolling, splashing sea
   I could see it rise and dip.

In the great dark sky above
   Stars were scattered everywhere,
Ships, I thought, were just like stars
   As I lay and watched them there.

For a world is every star
   In a heaven of its own:
Every ship a little world
   Out upon the sea alone.

Marjorie Wilson

THE JOURNEY

We are going on a journey,
   We are going all the way,
A-riding in a wagon
   On soft sweet-scented hay:
The Wagoner is waiting
   (A jolly coachman he)
To take us on our journey
   To a farm-house by the sea.
Our great big friends the horses
   Are joining in the fun,
A knowing look they're wearing
   While waiting in the sun;
It's such a jolly farm-house
   In the valley by the sea,
And the farmer's just as jolly
   As any man could be.
There isn't any hurry,
   The ride is splendid sport,
A wood, a windy common,
   Then a little sleepy port.
The farmer's wife is waiting,
   With strawberries for tea,
And cream and smiles of welcome,
   In the farm-house by the sea.
And when the day is over,
   All tired with sheer delight,
We'll climb up to our bedroom
   To sleep away the night
Where linen smells of lavender;
   Then waking full of glee,
We'll hear the farmer calling,
   And murmur of the sea.

Aidan Clarke

THE TRAIN

A green eye – and a red – in the dark,
Thunder – smoke – and a spark.

It is there – it is here – flashed by.
Whither will the wild thing fly?

It is rushing, tearing through the night,
Rending her gloom in its flight.

It shatters her silence with shrieks.
What is it the wild thing seeks?

Alas! for it hurries away
Them that are fain to stay.

Hurrah! for it carries home
Lovers and friends that roam.

Mary E. Coleridge

A KAYAK SONG

Over the dark water
  See the kayak steal;
Father's going searching
  For the fish and seal.

Will he have good hunting
  Out beyond the floe?
He may see a bear there
  'Mid the ice and snow.

If he gets a walrus.
  There will be for me
Thongs and reins for sledges
  Whips of ivory.

Over the dark water
  See the kayak steal
Softly – lest it frighten
  Hidden fish and seal.

Lucy Diamond

167

THE WINDOW CLEANER

A window cleaner's life is grand!
   Hurrying up his ladder-stair,
He sets himself with mop in hand
   To let in sunshine everywhere;
It makes me feel I'd like to be
   A window cleaner too, like him,
Taking my ladder round with me
   To get at windows dark and dim.

Having my polisher and mop
   On every dull and grimy pane,
I'd rub, and rub, and never stop
   Until I made them bright again;
I'd do the same by high and low,
   Making their glass so shiny-clean
That all who looked through it would know
   At once – the window-man had been!

Elizabeth Fleming

THE FLOWER-SELLER

The Flower-seller's fat, and she wears a big shawl!
She sits on the kerb with her basket and all;
The wares that she sells us are not very dear
And are always the loveliest things of the year.
      Daffodils in April,
        Purple flags in May,
      Sweet peas like butterflies
        Upon a summer day,
      Brown leaves in autumn,
        Green leaves in spring,
      And berries in the winter
        When the carol-singers sing.
The Flower-seller sits with her hands in her lap,
When she's not crying Roses, she's taking a nap;
Her bonnet is queer, and she calls you My dear,
And sells you the lovelist things of the year.

Eleanor Farjeon

THE SHEPHERD BOY

The shepherd boy a kingdom rules,
   An emerald hill his throne;
Crown'd with golden sunshine,
   He reigneth there alone.

His goats, court-players are;
   Each wears a tinkling bell,
And the birds' sweet pipings,
   A royal concert tell.

And the piping and the bells,
   With the brook's soft rhymes,
Lull the drowsy king to sleep,
   While gently nod the pines.

Heinrich Heine

TOPSY-TURVY LAND

The people walk upon their heads,
   The sea is made of sand,
The children go to school by night,
   In Topsy-Turvy Land,

The front-door step is at the back,
   You're walking when you stand,
You wear your hat upon your feet,
   In Topsy-Turvy Land.

And buses on the sea you'll meet,
   While pleasure boats are planned
To travel up and down the streets
   Of Topsy-Turvy Land.

You pay for what you never get,
   I think it must be grand,
For when you go you're coming back,
   In Topsy-Turvy Land.

H. E. Wilkinson

SHINING THINGS

I love all shining things —
                    The lovely moon
The silver stars at night,
                    gold sun at noon.
A glowing rainbow in
                    a stormy sky,
Or bright clouds hurrying
                    when wind goes by.

I love the glow-worm's elf-light
                    in the lane,
And leaves a-shine with glistening
                    drops of rain,
The glinting wings of bees,
                    and butterflies,
My purring pussy's green
                    and shining eyes.

I love the street-lamps shining
                    through the gloom,
Tall candles lighted in
                    a shadowy room,
New-tumbled chestnuts from
                    the chestnut tree,
And gleaming fairy bubbles
                    blown by me.

I love the shining buttons
                    on my coat,
I love the bright beads round
                    my mother's throat,
I love the coppery flames
                    of red and gold,
That cheer and comfort me
                    when I'm a-cold.

The beauty of all shining things
                    is yours and mine,
It was a *lovely* thought of God
                    to make things shine.

                                        Elizabeth Gould

170

THE OLD KITCHEN CLOCK

Listen to the Kitchen Clock,
To itself it ever talks,
From its place it never walks;
'Tick-tock – tick-tock,'
Tell me what it says.

'I'm a very patient clock,
Never moved by hope or fear,
Though I've stood for many a year;
Tick-tock – tick-tock,'
That is what it says.

'I'm a very truthful clock;
People say, about the place,
Truth is written on my face;
Tick-tock – tick-tock,'
That is what it says.

'I'm a very active clock,
For I go while you're asleep,
Though you never take a peep.
Tick-tock – tick-tock,'
That is what it says.

'I'm a most obliging clock;
If you wish to hear me strike,
You may do it when you like;
Tick-tock – tick-tock,'
That is what it says.

What a talkative old clock!
Let us see what it will do
When the pointer reaches two.
'Ding-ding – tick-tock.'
That is what it says.

Ann Hawkshawe

FROM A RAILWAY CARRIAGE

Faster than fairies, faster than witches,
Bridges and houses, hedges and ditches;
And charging along like troops in a battle,
All through the meadows the horses and cattle;
All of the sights of the hill and the plain
Fly as thick as driving rain;
And ever again, in the wink of an eye,
Painted stations whistle by.

Here is a child who clambers and scrambles,
All by himself and gathering brambles;
Here is a tramp who stands and gazes;
And there is the green for stringing the daisies!
Here is a cart run away in the road
Lumping along with man and load;
And here is a mill, and there is a river:
Each a glimpse and gone for ever!

Robert Louis Stevenson

CARAVANS

I've seen caravans
Going to the fair!
Come along,
Come along;
Let's go there!

Hurrah! roundabouts,
Lovely little swings,
Coconuts,
Coconuts,
Heaps of things!

See all the animals
Waiting for the show
Elephants,
Elephants,
Let's all go!

Look! There's a tiger
Watching baby bears;
Come away,
Come away,
How he stares!

Hark! how the music plays
Ready for the fun!
Come along,
Come along,
Let's all run.

Irene Thompson

NO THOROUGHFARE

In a dear little home of tarpaulin and boards,
   Where the wood-blocks are 'up' in our street,
Lives a little old man dressed in sacking and cords,
   Crouching snug on a low wooden seat.

There's a brazier of charcoal that flickers and glows
   Where the wigwam's front door ought to be;
As the little old man toasts his fingers and nose,
   How I wish he had room there for me!

I could hang out the lanterns on trestles and poles,
   Like big rubies all shining and red,
And to guard a wide street full of wood-blocks and holes
   Is far nicer than going to bed.

I could stay all night long by the little old man
   Keeping watch o'er each pickaxe and spade,
Frying sausages too, in a battered old pan,
   For the dark would not make me afraid.

And the little old man might drop off in a doze
   Till the sky turned to orange and pink,
But the street would be safe from all brigands and foes
   For *I* should not have slumbered a wink.

Ruth Holmes

PLAYGROUNDS

In summer I am very glad
  We children are so small,
For we can see a thousand things
  That men can't see at all.

They don't know much about the moss
  And all the stones they pass:
They never lie and play among
  The forests in the grass:

They walk about a long way off:
  And, when we're at the sea,
Let father stoop as best he can
  He can't find things like me.

But, when the snow is on the ground
  And all the puddles freeze,
I wish that I were very tall,
  High up above the trees.

L. Alma Tadema

SHELL SECRETS

Tell me your secrets, pretty shell,
I will promise not to tell!

Humming, hummming, soft and low —
All about the sea, I know.

You are murmuring, I think,
Of the sea-weeds, green and pink,

Of the tiny baby shells
Where the mother mermaid dwells,

Pretty shell, I'm waiting here,
Come and whisper in my ear.

'SOOEEP!'

Black as a chimney is his face,
    And ivory white his teeth,
And in his brass-bound cart he rides,
    The chestnut blooms beneath.

'Sooeep, Sooeep!' he cries, and brightly peers
    This way and that to see
With his two light-blue shining eyes
    What custom there may be.

And once inside the house, he'll squat,
    And drive his rods on high,
Till twirls his sudden sooty brush
    Against the morning sky.

Then 'mid his bulging bags of soot,
    With half the world asleep,
His small cart wheels him off again,
    Still hoarsely bawling, 'Sooeep!'

Walter de la Mare

THE CLOTHES-LINE

Hand in hand they dance in a row,
Hither and thither, and to and fro,
Flip! Flap! Flop! and away they go —
Flutt'ring creatures as white as snow,
Like restive horses they caper and prance;
Like fairy-tale witches they wildly dance;
Rounded in front, but hollow behind,
They shiver and skip in the merry March wind.
One I saw dancing excitedly,
Struggling so wildly till she was free,
Then, leaving pegs and clothes-line behind her
She flew like a bird, and no one can find her.
I saw her gleam, like a sail, in the sun,
Flipping and flapping and flopping for fun.
Nobody knows where she now can be,
Hid in a ditch, or drowned in the sea.
She was my handkerchief not long ago,
But she'll never come back to my pocket, I know.

Charlotte Druitt Cole

DANNY MURPHY

He was as old as old could be,
His little eye could scarcely see,
His mouth was sunken in between
His nose and chin, and he was lean
And twisted up and withered quite,
So that he couldn't walk aright.

His pipe was always going out,
And then he'd have to search about
In all his pockets, and he'd mow —
O deary me! and, musha now!
And then he'd light his pipe, and then
He'd let it go clean out again.

He couldn't dance or jump or run,
Or ever have a bit of fun
Like me and Susan, when we shout
And jump and throw ourselves about —
But when he laughed, then you could see
He was as young as young could be!

James Stephens

BREAD

'Farmer, is the harvest ready
 For we must have bread?'
'Go and look at all my fields,'
 Is what the farmer said.

So we ran and saw the wheat
 Standing straight and tall.
'There's your bread,' the farmer said,
 'Have no fear at all.'

'Miller, is the flour ready
 For we must have bread?'
'Go and look in all my sacks.'
 Is what the miller said.

So we ran and saw the flour,
   Soft and white as snow.
'There's your flour,' the miller said,
   As we turned to go.

'Mother, is the oven ready
   For we must have bread?'
'Go and open wide the door,'
   Is what our mother said.

So we ran and saw the loaves
   Crisp and brown to see.
'There's your bread,' our mother said,
   'Ready for your tea.'

H. E. Wilkinson

CHIMNEY-TOPS

Ah! the morning is grey;
And what kind of day
Is it likely to be?
You must look up and see
What the chimney-tops say.

If the smoke from the mouth
Of the chimney goes south,
'Tis the north wind that blows
From the country of snows;
Look out for rough weather.
The cold and the north wind
Are always together.

If the smoke pouring forth
From the chimney goes north,
A mild day it will be,
A warm time we shall see;
The south wind is blowing
From lands where the orange
And fig trees are growing.

THE OLD WOMAN OF THE ROADS

O, to have a little house!
  To own the hearth and stool and all!
The heaped-up sods upon the fire,
  The pile of turf against the wall!

To have a clock with weights and chains
  And pendulum swinging up and down!
A dresser filled with shining delph,
  Speckled and white and blue and brown!

I could be busy all the day
  Clearing and sweeping hearth and floor
And fixing on their shelf again
  My white and blue and speckled store!

I could be quiet there at night,
  Beside the fire and by myself,
Sure of a bed; and loth to leave
  The ticking clock and the shining delph!

Oh! but I'm weary of mist and dark,
  And roads where there's never a house or bush,
And tired I am of the bog, and the road,
  And the crying wind and the lonesome hush!

And I am praying to God on high,
  And I am praying Him night and day,
For a little house – a house of my own —
  Out of the wind's and the rain's way.

Padraic Colum

VACATION TIME

Good-bye, little desk at school, good-bye,
We're off to the fields and the open sky.
The bells of the brooks and the woodland bells
Are ringing us out to the vales and dells,
To meadow-ways fair, and to hilltops cool,
Good-bye, little desk at school.

Good-bye, little desk at school, good-bye,
We've other brave lessons and tasks to try;
But we shall come back in the fall, you know,
And as gay to come as we are to go,
With ever a laugh and never a sigh —
Good-bye, little desk, good-bye!

Frank Hutt

A RHYME SHEET OF OTHER LANDS

The Japanese have funny things
    For dinner, so they say;
The tails of fish and dragon's wings
    Are eaten every day.

Of all the men who search for gold,
    Some find as much of it
As both their restless hands can hold,
    And others ne'er a bit.

I think this picture here shall be
    The famous river Nile
And, lying near the bank, you see
    The curious crocodile.

The Greeks of old were wise and skilled,
    What wonders they could do!
What towns and temples they could build,
    And stately houses, too!

Now every child in China knows
    The way to spell and write with speed;
From right to left the writing goes —
    It must be very hard indeed!

I'd love to go to Switzerland,
    Although the air is colder:
There's little doubt that it's a land
    I'll go to when I'm older.

Hugh Chesterman

179

THE SONG OF THE BATH

Bring the biggest bath you've seen,
Water hot and towels clean,
Bring the soap that smells so sweetly;
Bring the nighties, folded neatly —
Bath time! Bath time! Hip hooray!
Jolliest time of all the day!

Bring the funny rubber toys,
Bring the little girls and boys;
Sticky fingers, grubby knees,
Rub them, scrub them, if you please.
Bath time! Bath time! Work away —
Busiest time of all the day.

Bring the grumbles and complainings,
Bring the little aches and painings,
All the frowns and all the tears,
Drown them in the bath, my dears.
Bath time! Bath time! Kiss, and say,
Happiest time of all the day!

Margaret Gibbs

THE LITTLE DANCERS
A London Vision

Lonely, save for a few faint stars, the sky
Dreams; and lonely, below, the little street
Into its gloom retires, secluded and shy.
Scarcely the dumb roar enters this soft retreat;
And all is dark, save where come flooding rays
From a tavern window: there to the brisk measure
Of an organ that down in an alley merrily plays,
Two children, all alone and no one by,
Holding their tatter'd frocks, through an airy maze
Of motion, lightly threaded with nimble feet,
Dance sedately; face to face they gaze,
Their eyes shining, grave with a perfect pleasure.

Laurence Binyon

ON THE BANISTERS

Sliding down the banisters,
  The day it rained all day,
We played at flying fairies
  Coming down a rainbow ray.
I slit my frock a little bit,
  And Billy tore the mat —
But fairies aren't particular
  About such things as that.

Sliding down the banisters
  The day it rained all day,
We played at sailing aeroplanes
  To countries miles away.
I hurt my hand a little bit,
  And Billy bumped his nose,
But airmen take no notice,
  Of such little things as those.

Sliding down the banisters
  The day it rained all day,
We played at swings and switchbacks
  Like they have Olympia way.
Then folks came in, all wet and cross,
  And made us stop our play.
But oh, we did enjoy ourselves
  The day it rained all day.

Margaret E. Gibbs

THE KITE

I wonder what my kite can see,
So high above the world and me;
And if the birds are friends to him,
As I am friends with Jack and Jim,
And are the clouds just really rain,
That melts and pours all down again?
O! he must know a thousand things,
As much as schoolmasters, and kings;
But will he breathe a word to me?
No, he's as quiet as quiet can be.

Pearl Forbes MacEwen

THE SHELL

See what a lovely shell,
Small and pure as a pearl,
Lying close to my foot,
Frail, but a work divine,
Made so fairly well
With delicate spire and whorl,
How exquisitely minute,
A miracle of design!

What is it? a learnèd man
Could give it a clumsy name.
Let him name it who can,
The beauty would be the same.

The tiny cell is forlorn,
Void of the little living will
That made it stir on the shore.
Did he stand at the diamond door
Of his house in a rainbow frill?
Did he push, when he was uncurl'd,
A golden foot or fairy horn
Thro' his dim water-world?

Slight, to be crush'd with a tap
Of my finger-nail on the sand;
Small, but a work divine,
Frail, but of force to withstand,
Year upon year, the shock
Of cataract seas that snap
The three-decker's oaken spine
Athwart the ledges of rock,
Here on the Breton strand!

Lord Tennyson

MOONLIT APPLES

At the top of the house the apples are laid in rows,
And the skylight lets the moonlight in, and those
Apples are deep-sea apples of green. There goes
   A cloud on the moon in the autumn night.

A mouse in the wainscot scratches, and scratches, and then
There is no sound at the top of the house of men
Or mice; and the cloud is blown, and the moon again
  Dapples the apples with deep-sea light.

They are lying in rows there, under the bloomy beams;
On the sagging floor; they gather the silver streams
Out of the moon, those moonlit apples of dreams,
  And quiet is the steep stair under.

In the corridors under there is nothing but sleep.
And stiller than ever on orchard boughs they keep
Tryst with the moon, and deep in the silence, deep
  On moon-washed apples of wonder.

John Drinkwater

WHEN ALL THE WORLD IS YOUNG

When all the world is young, lad,
  And all the trees are green;
And every goose a swan, lad,
  And every lass a queen;
Then hey for boot and horse, lad,
  And round the world away;
Young blood must have its course, lad,
  And every dog his day.

When all the world is old, lad,
  And all the trees are brown;
And all the sport is stale, lad,
  And all the wheels run down:
Creep home, and take your place there,
  The spent and maimed among:
God grant you find one face there
  You love when all was young.

Charles Kingsley

FOUR AND EIGHT

The Foxglove by the cottage door
Looks down on Joe, and Joe is four.

The Foxglove by the garden gate
Looks down on Joan, and Joan is eight.

'I'm glad we're small,' said Joan, 'I love
To see inside the fox's glove,
Where taller people cannot see,
And all is ready for the bee;
The door is wide, the feast is spread,
The walls are dotted rosy red.'
'And only little people know
How nice it looks in there,' said Joe.
Said Joan, 'The upper rooms are locked;
A bee went buzzing up – he knocked,
But no one let him in, so then
He bumbled gaily down again.'
'Oh dear!' sighed Joe, 'if only we
Could grow as little as that bee,
We too might room by room explore
The Foxglove by the cottage door.'

The Foxglove by the garden gate
Looked down and smiled on Four and Eight.

ffrida Wolfe

LITTLE RAIN-DROPS

Oh, where do you come from,
   You little drops of rain,
Pitter, patter, pitter, patter,
   Down the window-pane?

They won't let me walk,
   And they won't let me play,
And they won't let me go
   Out of doors at all today.

They put away my playthings
  Because I broke them all,
And then they locked all up my bricks,
  And took away my ball.

Tell me, little rain-drops,
  Is that the way you play,
Pitter, patter, pitter, patter,
  All the rainy day?

They say I'm very naughty,
  But I've nothing else to do
But sit here at the window:
  I should like to play with you.

The little rain-drops cannot speak,
  But 'Pitter, patter, pat,'
Means 'We can play on *this* side,
  Why can't you play on *that*?'

Ann Hawkshawe

A FEATHER FOR MY CAP

Seagull flying from the sea,
Drop a feather here for me!
Drop it down into my lap —
I need a feather for my cap!

My satin gown's as white as milk,
My stockings are the finest silk,
My shoes are made of Spanish leather,
But oh! my cap! it lacks a feather!

My girdle is of precious gold,
A bouquet in my hands I hold
Of wild rose buds and lucky heather —
But oh! my cap! it lacks a feather!

What use a gown of satin fine?
What use a grand bouquet – like mine?
What use are shoes of Spanish leather
If caps, or hats, do lack a feather?

Ivy O. Eastwick

THE COBBLER

Wandering up and down one day,
I peeped into a window over the way;
And putting his needle through and through,
There sat a cobbler making a shoe:
For the world he cares never the whisk of a broom —
All he wants is elbow-room.
    Rap-a-tap-tap, tick-a-tack-too,
    That is the way he makes a shoe!

Over laths of wood his bits of leather
He stretches and fits, then sews together;
He puts his wax ends through and through;
And still as he stitches, his body goes too:
For the world he cares never the whisk of a broom —
All he wants is elbow-room.
    Rap-a-tap-tap, tick-a-tack-too,
    This is the way he makes a shoe!

With his little sharp awl he makes a hole
Right through the upper and through the sole;
He puts in one peg, and he puts in two,
And chuckles and laughs as he hammers them through:
For the world he cares never the whisk of a broom —
All he wants is elbow-room.
    Rap-a-tap-tap, tick-a-tack-too,
    This is the way to make a shoe!

THE NIGHT WILL NEVER STAY

The night will never stay,
    The night will still go by,
Though with a million stars
    You pin it to the sky,
Though you bind it with the blowing wind
    And buckle it with the moon,
The night will slip away
    Like sorrow or a tune.

Eleanor Farjeon

THE SPEED TRACK

The Hour-hand and the Minute-hand upon a polished dial
A meeting planned at twelve o'clock to walk and talk awhile.
The Hour-hand with the Minute-hand could never keep apace.
'The speed at which you move,' he said, 'is really a disgrace!'

Then laughed the Minute-hand and sang, 'The way that I must go
Is marked with milestones all along, and there are twelve, you know.
And I must call at each of these before my journey's done,
While you are creeping like a snail from twelve o'clock to one.
So now, farewell! But we shall meet again, good sir,' said he,
'The road that we are following is circular, you see!'

'Peter'

THE WITCH

I saw her plucking cowslips,
    And marked her where she stood:
She never knew I watched her
    While hiding in the wood.

Her skirt was brightest crimson,
    And black her steeple hat,
Her broomstick lay beside her —
    I'm positive of that.

Her chin was sharp and pointed,
    Her eyes were – I don't know —
For, when she turned towards me —
    I thought it best – to go!

Percy H. Ilott

HAPPY THOUGHT

The world is so full of a number of things,
I'm sure we should all be as happy as kings.

Robert Louis Stevenson

WATER

Water has no taste at all,
   Water has no smell;
Water's in the waterfall,
   In pump, and tap, and well.

Water's everywhere about;
   Water's in the rain,
In the bath, the pond, and out
   At sea it's there again.

Water comes into my eyes
   And down my cheeks in tears,
When mother cries, 'Go back and try
   To wash behind those ears.'

John R. Crossland

GOLDENHAIR

Lean out of the window,
   Goldenhair,
I heard you singing
   A merry air.

My book is closed;
   I read no more,
Watching the fire dance
   On the floor.

I have left my book;
   I have left my room,
For I heard you singing
   Through the gloom.

Singing and singing
   A merry air,
Lean out of the window.
Goldenhair.

James Joyce

Fables and Stories – Grave and Gay

PART SEVEN

Such wondrous tales as childhood loves to hear

THE NEW DUCKLING

'I want to be new,' said the duckling.
  'O, ho!' said the wise old owl,
While the guinea-pig cluttered off chuckling
  To tell all the rest of the fowl.

'I should like a more elegant figure,'
  That child of a duck went on.
'I should like to grow bigger and bigger,
  Until I could swallow a swan.

'I won't be the bond-slave of habit,
  I won't have those webs on my toes,
I want to run round as a rabbit,
  A rabbit as red a rose.

'I don't want to waddle like mother,
  Or quack like my silly old dad.
I want to be utterly other,
  And frightfully modern and mad.'

'Do you know,' said the turkey, 'you're quacking!
  There's a fox creeping up thro' the rye:
And, if you're not utterly lacking,
  You'll make for that duck-pond. Good-bye.'

But the duckling was perky as perky.
  'Take care of your stuffing!' he called.
(This was horribly rude to a turkey!)
  'But you aren't a real turkey,' he bawled.

'You're an early Victorian sparrow!
  A fox is more fun than a sheep!
I shall show that my mind is not narrow
  And give him my feathers – to keep.'

Now the curious end of this fable,
  So far as the rest ascertained,
Though they searched from the barn to the stable,
  Was that only his feathers remained.

So he wasn't the bond-slave of habit,
   And he didn't have webs on his toes;
And perhaps he runs round like a rabbit,
   A rabbit as red as a rose.

Alfred Noyes

THE OWL AND THE PUSSY-CAT

The Owl and the Pussy-Cat went to sea
   In a beautiful pea-green boat.
They took some honey, and plenty of money,
   Wrapped up in a five-pound note.
The Owl looked up to the stars above,
   And sang to a small guitar,
'O lovely Pussy! O Pussy, my love,
   What a beautiful Pussy you are,
         You are!
   What a beautiful Pussy you are!'

Pussy said to the Owl, 'You elegant fowl!
   How charmingly sweet you sing!
O let us be married! too long we have tarried:
   But what shall we do for a ring?'
They sailed away for a year and a day,
   To the land where the Bong-tree grows,
And there in a wood a Piggy-wig stood,
   With a ring at the end of his nose,
         His nose,
   With a ring at the end of his nose.

'Dear Pig, are you willing to sell for one shilling
   Your ring?' said the Piggy, 'I will.'
So they took it away, and were married next day
   By the Turkey who lives on the hill.
They dined on mince, and slices of quince,
   Which they ate with a runcible spoon;
And hand in hand, on the edge of the sand,
   They danced by the light of the moon.

Edward Lear

THE FROG AND THE BIRD

By a quiet little stream on an old mossy log,
Looking very forlorn, sat a little green frog;
He'd a sleek speckled back, and two bright yellow eyes,
And when dining, selected the choicest of flies.

The sun was so hot he scarce opened his eyes,
Far too lazy to stir, let alone watch for flies,
He was nodding, and nodding, and almost asleep,
When a voice in the branches chirped: 'Froggie, cheep, cheep!'

'You'd better take care,' piped the bird to the frog,
'In the water you'll be if you fall off that log.
Can't you see that the streamlet is up to the brim?'
Croaked the froggie; 'What odds! You forget I can swim!'

Then the froggie looked up at the bird perched so high
On a bough that to him seemed to reach to the sky;
So he croaked to the bird: 'If you fall, you will die!'
Chirped the birdie: 'What odds! You forget I can fly!'

Vera Hessey

A TRAGIC STORY

There lived a sage in days of yore,
And he a handsome pigtail wore:
But wondered much and sorrowed more
  Because it hung behind him.

He mused upon this curious case,
And swore he'd change the pigtail's place,
And have it hanging at his face,
  Not dangling there behind him.

Says he, 'The mystery I've found —
I'll turn me round' – he turned him round;
  But still it hung behind him.

Then round, and round, and out and in,
All day the puzzled sage did spin;
In vain – it mattered not a pin —
  The pigtail hung behind him.

And right and left, and round about,
And up and down, and in and out,
He turned; but still the pigtail stout
  Hung steadily behind him.

And though his efforts never slack,
And though he twist, and twirl, and tack,
Alas! still faithful to his back,
  The pigtail hangs behind him.

W. M. Thackeray

JACK O' THE INKPOT

I dance on your paper,
  I hide in your pen,
I make in your ink-stand
  My little black den;
And when you're not looking
  I hop on your nose,
And leave on your forehead
  The marks of my toes.

When you're trying to finish
  Your 'i' with a dot,
I slip down your finger
  And make it a blot;
And when you're so busy
  To cross a big 'T',
I make on the paper
  A little Black Sea.

I drink blotting-paper,
  Eat penwiper pie,
You never can catch me,
  You never need try!
I leap any distance,
  I use any ink,
I'm on to your fingers
  Before you can wink.

Algernon Blackwood

THE WONDERFUL DERBY RAM

As I was going to Derby, all on a market day,
I met the finest ram, sir, that ever was fed upon hay,
        Upon hay, upon hay, upon hay;
I met the finest ram, sir, that ever was fed upon hay.

This ram was fat behind, sir, this ram was fat before,
This ram was ten yards round, sir, indeed he was no more,
        No more, no more, no more;
This ram was ten yards round, sir, indeed he was no more.

The horns that grew on his head, sir, they were so wondrous high,
As I've been plainly told, sir, they reached up to the sky,
        The sky, the sky, the sky;
As I've been plainly told, sir, they reached up to the sky.

The tail that grew from his back, sir, was six yards and an ell,
And it was sent to Derby to toll the market bell,
        The bell, the bell, the bell;
And it was sent to Derby to toll the market bell.

JUST LIKE A MAN

He sat at the dinner table
  With a discontented frown,
The potatoes and steak were underdone
  And the bread was baked too brown;
The pie was too sour and the pudding too sweet,
  And the roast was much too fat;
The soup so greasy, too, and salt,
  'Twas hardly fit for the cat.

'I wish you could eat the bread and pie
  I've seen my mother make,
They are something like, and 'twould do you good
  Just to look at a loaf of her cake.'
Said the smiling wife, 'I'll improve with age —
  Just now I'm but a beginner;
But your mother has come to visit us,
  And today she cooked the dinner.'

YUSSOUF

A stranger came one night to Yussouf's tent,
  Saying – 'Behold one outcast and in dread,
Against whose life the bow of Power is bent,
  Who flies, and hath not where to lay his head.
I come to thee for shelter and for food:
To Yussouf, call'd through all our tribes the Good.'

'This tent is mine,' said Yussouf – 'but no more
  Than it is God's: come in and be at peace;
Freely shalt thou partake of all my store,
  As I of His who buildeth over these
Our tents His glorious roof of night and day,
And at whose door none ever yet heard Nay.'

So Yussouf entertain'd his guest that night;
  And waking him ere day, said – 'Here is gold;
My swiftest horse is saddled for thy flight —
  Depart before the prying day grow bold!'
As one lamp lights another, nor grows less,
So nobleness enkindleth nobleness.

That inward light the stranger's face made grand
  Which shines from all self-conquest; kneeling low;
He bow'd his forehead upon Yussouf's hand,
  Sobbing – 'O Sheikh! I cannot leave thee so —
I will repay thee – all this thou hast done
Unto that Ibrahim who slew thy son!'

'Take thrice the gold!' said Yussouf – 'for with thee
  Into the desert, never to return,
My one black thought shall ride away from me.
  First-born, for whom by day and night I yearn,
Balanced and just are all of God's decrees;
Thou art avenged, my First-born! sleep in peace!'

J. R. Lowell

THE WRAGGLE TAGGLE GIPSIES

There were three gipsies a-come to my door,
  And downstairs ran this lady, O!
One sang high, and another sang low,
  And the other sang, Bonny, bonny, Biscay, O!

Then she pulled off her silk finished gown
  And put on hose of leather, O!
The ragged, ragged rags about our door —
  She's gone with the wraggle taggle gipsies, O!

It was late last night, when my lord came home,
  Enquiring for his a-lady, O!
The servants said on every hand:
  'She's gone with the wraggle taggle gispies, O!'

'O saddle to me my milk-white steed,
  Go and fetch me my pony, O!
That I may ride and seek my bride,
  Who is gone with the wraggle taggle gipsies, O!'

O he rode high and he rode low,
  He rode through woods and copses too,
Until he came to an open field,
  And there he espied his a-lady, O!

'What makes you leave your house and land?
  What makes you leave your money, O?
What makes you leave your new-wedded lord;
  To go with the wraggle taggle gipsies, O?'

'What care I for my house and my land?
  What care I for my money, O?
What care I for my new-wedded lord?
  I'm off with the wraggle taggle gipsies, O!'

'Last night you slept on a goose-feather bed,
  With the sheet turned down so bravely, O!
And tonight you'll sleep in a cold open field,
  Along with the wraggle taggle gipsies, O!'

'What care I for a goose-feather bed,
  With the sheet turned down so bravely, O!
For tonight I shall sleep in a cold open field,
  Along with the wraggle taggle gipsies, O!'

BETTY AT THE PARTY

'When I was at the party,'
  Said Betty, aged just four,
'A little girl fell off her chair
  Right down upon the floor;
And all the other little girls
  Began to laugh, but me —
I didn't laugh a single bit,'
  Said Betty seriously.

'Why not?' her mother asked her,
  Full of delight to find
That Betty – bless her little heart! —
  Had been so sweetly kind.
'Why didn't you laugh, my darling?
  Or don't you like to tell?'
'I didn't laugh,' said Betty,
  ''Cause it was me that fell.'

From A SONG ABOUT MYSELF

There was a naughty boy,
  A naughty boy was he,
He would not stop at home,
  He could not quiet be —
      He took
      In his knapsack
      A Book
      Full of vowels,
      And a shirt
      With some towels —
      A slight cap
      For night cap —
      A hair brush,
      Comb ditto,
      New stockings,
      For old ones
      Would split O!
      This knapsack
      Tight at 'a back
      He riveted close
And followed his nose
      To the North,
      To the North,
And followed his nose
      To the North.

There was a naughty boy,
  And a naughty boy was he,
For nothing would he do
  But scribble poetry —
      He took
      An inkstand
      In his hand
      And a Pen
      Big as ten
      In the other,
      And away

In a pother
He ran
To the mountains
And fountains
And ghostes
And witches
And ditches
And wrote
In his coat
When the weather
Was cool
Fearing gout,
And without
When the weather
Was warm —
O the charm
When we choose
To follow one's nose
To the North,
To the North,
To follow one's nose
To the North!

These delightful nonsense verses were written by John Keats to amuse his littl sister. Playing with words is a game which amuses many children and some ma like to write their own nonsense verses after hearing these.

THE LOBSTER QUADRILLE

'Will you walk a little faster?' said a whiting to a snail,
'There's a porpoise close behind us, and he's treading on my tail.
See how eagerly the lobsters and the turtles all advance!
They are waiting on the shingle – will you come and join the dance?
Will you, won't you, will you, won't you, will you join the dance?
Will you, won't you, will you, won't you, won't you join the dance?

'You can really have no notion how delightful it will be,
When they take us up and throw us, with the lobsters, out to sea!'
But the snail replied, 'Too far, too far!' and gave a look askance,
Said he thanked the whiting kindly, but he would not join the dance,
　　Would not, could not, would not, could not, would not join the dance
　　Would not, could not, would not, could not, could not join the dance.

'What matters it how far we go?' his scaly friend replied.
'There is another shore, you know, upon the other side.
The further off from England the nearer is to France —
Then turn not pale, beloved snail, but come and join the dance.
　　Will you, won't you, will you, won't you, will you join the dance?
　　Will you, won't you, will you, won't you, won't you join the dance?'

Lewis Carroll

THE JOVIAL BEGGAR

There was a jovial beggar,
　　He had a wooden leg,
Lame from his cradle,
　　And forced for to beg.
And a-begging we will go, will go, will go,
　　And a-begging we will go!

A bag for his oatmeal,
　　Another for his salt,
And a pair of crutches,
　　To show that he can halt.
And a-begging we will go —

A bag for his wheat,
　　Another for his rye,
A little bottle by his side,
　　To drink when he's a-dry,
And a-begging we will go —

'Seven years I begged
　　For my old Master Wild,
He taught me to beg
　　When I was but a child,
And a-begging we will go —

'I begged for my master
　　And got him store of pelf;
But, now, Jove be praised!
　　I'm begging for myself;
And a-begging we will go —

'In a hollow tree
　　I live and pay no rent.
Providence provides for me,
　　And I am well content;
And a-begging we will go —

'Of all the occupations
　　A beggar's life is best,
For whenever he's a-weary
　　He'll lay him down and rest
And a-begging we will go —

'I fear no plots against me,
　　I live in open cell;
Then who would be a king,
　　When beggars live so well?
Then a-begging we will go, will go, will go,
　　And a-begging we will go!'

MOUNTAIN AND THE SQUIRREL

The Mountain and the Squirrel
Had a quarrel,
And the former call'd the latter 'Little Prig';
Bun replied,
'You are doubtless very big,
But all sorts of things and weather
Must be taken in together
To make up a year
And a sphere.
And I think it no disgrace
To occupy my place.
If I'm not so large as you,
You are not so small as I,
And not half so spry;
I'll not deny you make
A very pretty squirrel-track;
Talents differ; all is well and wisely put;
If I cannot carry forests on my back,
Neither can you crack a nut.'

Ralph Waldo Emerson

THE BLIND MEN AND THE ELEPHANT

It was six men of Hindostan,
    To learning much inclined,
Who went to see the elephant,
    (Though all of them were blind):
That each by observation
    Might satisfy his mind.

The *first* approached the Elephant,
    And happening to fall
Against his broad and sturdy side,
    At once began to bawl:
'Bless me, it seems the Elephant
    Is very like a wall.'

The *second*, feeling of his tusk,
　Cried, 'Ho! what have we here
So very round and smooth and sharp?
　To me 'tis mighty clear
This wonder of an Elephant
　Is very like a spear.'

The *third* approached the animal,
　And happening to take
The squirming trunk within his hands,
　Then boldly up and spake:
'I see,' quoth he, 'the Elephant
　Is very like a snake.'

The *fourth* stretched out his eager hand
　And felt about the knee,
'What most this mighty beast is like
　Is mighty plain,' quoth he;
''Tis clear enough the Elephant
　Is very like a tree.'

The *fifth* who chanced to touch the ear
　Said, 'Even the blindest man
Can tell what this resembles most;
　Deny the fact who can,
This marvel of an Elephant
　Is very like a fan.'

The *sixth* no sooner had begun
　About the beast to grope,
Than, seizing the swinging tail
　That fell within his scope,
'I see,' cried he, 'the Elephant
　Is very like a rope.'

And so these men of Hindostan
　Disputed loud and long,
Each in his own opinion
　Exceeding stiff and strong,
Though *each* was *partly* in the right
　And all were in the wrong.

John Godfrey Saxe

203

SONS OF THE KING

A little Prince of long ago
   The day that he was six
Put away his birthday toys,
   His soldiers, trains and bricks.

And stealing down the golden stair,
   His slippers in his hand,
He from the shady courtyard stepped
   Into a sunlit land.

And sitting there beside the wall
   He buttoned up his shoes
And wondered – looking up and down —
   Which highway should he choose.

When by there rode a gipsy boy,
   His pony dark as he,
Who smiled upon the little Prince
   So golden-fair to see.

'Where are you riding, gipsy boy,
   This lovely summer day?'
'Over the hills and through the woods
   To the land of Far-Away.'

'Who is your father, gipsy boy?
   For mine, you know, is king,
And I shall be like him one day
   And wear his crown and ring.'

'My father,' said the gipsy boy,
   'He also is a king.
Although he sits upon no throne
   And wears no crown or ring.

'He's king of all the gipsy-folk
    Twixt here and Far-Away,
And I, who am his eldest son,
    Shall be a king some day.'

'May I go with you, gipsy boy,
    To ride your little horse,
To see your tents and caravans
    Between the golden gorse?

'There I could run without my shoes
    And climb your forest trees,
I seem to smell your smoky fires
    Of crackling twigs and leaves.'

Within the Palace voices call,
    The gates are opened wide,
The kindly watchmen see the Prince
    And beckon him inside.

The gipsy smiles and shakes his head,
    He jerks the pony's rein;
'When you and I are kings,' he says,
    'Then we shall meet again.'

Joan Agnew

MR NOBODY

I know a funny little man,
    As quiet as a mouse,
Who does the mischief that is done
    In everybody's house!
There's no one ever sees his face,
    And yet we all agree
That every plate we break was cracked
    By Mr Nobody.

'Tis he who always tears our books,
    Who leaves the door ajar,
He pulls the buttons from our shirts,
    And scatters pins afar;
That squeaking door will always squeak,
    For, prithee, don't you see,
We leave the oiling to be done
    By Mr Nobody.

He puts damp wood upon the fire,
    That kettle cannot boil;
His are the feet that bring in the mud,
    And all the carpets soil.
The papers always are mislaid,
    Who had them last but he?
There's not one tosses them about
    But Mr Nobody.

The finger-marks upon the door
    By none of us are made;
We never leave the blinds unclosed,
    To let the curtains fade;
The ink we never spill; the boots
    That lying round you see
Are not our boots; they all belong
    To Mr Nobody.

THE PIRATES' TEA-PARTY

We'd ever so many kinds of cake
  And at least three sorts of jam.
Doughnuts and cucumber sandwiches,
  Some made with chicken and ham,
Scones and parkin and honey had we
The day that the pirates came to tea.

The oldest, he had twinkly eyes,
   A deep sword-slash on his cheek,
A stubbly beard that was nearly red,
   He hadn't washed for a week.
He showed me his cutlass sharp and bright,
He slept with it 'tween his teeth at night.

The second, he was thin and fair,
   He blushed when they yelled at him;
Tho' young he had killed a dozen Turks,
   They called him 'Terrible Tim'.
He wore a handkerchief round his head,
Purple and yellow with spots of red.

The third of the crew was extra tall,
   He knew many foreign parts,
He knew some wonderful swearing words,
   He understood all the charts,
But he only whispered one – when he found
His toast with the buttery side on the ground.

The fourth was merely a boy from a school,
   And altho' he wore a belt,
A pistol in it and high sea-boots,
   And a frightful hat of felt,
He is just pretending that he is one
With his 'Yo, ho, ho' and 'Son of a gun!'

If he is a pirate, I'm one too;
   Says he, 'Then be one quick;
Remember whatever the weather's like
   A pirate's never sea-sick.'
When the pirates came I wished that we
Had not asked that hateful boy to tea.

Dorothy Una Ratcliffe

GODFREY GORDON GUSTAVUS GORE

Godfrey Gordon Gustavus Gore —
No doubt you have heard that name before —
Was a boy who never would shut a door!

The wind might whistle, the wind might roar,
And teeth be aching and throats be sore,
But still he never would shut the door.

His father would beg, his mother implore,
'Godfrey Gordon Gustavus Gore,
We really do wish you would shut the door!'

Their hands they wrung, their hair they tore;
But Godfrey Gordon Gustavus Gore
Was as deaf as the buoy out at the Nore.

When he walked forth the folks would roar,
'Godfrey Gordon Gustavus Gore,
Why don't you think to shut the door?'

They rigged out a shutter with sail and oar,
And threatened to pack off Gustavus Gore
On a voyage of penance to Singapore.

But he begged for mercy, and said, 'No more!
Pray do not send me to Singapore
On a shutter, and then I will shut the door!'

THE TALE OF A DOG AND A BEE

Great big dog,
  Head upon his toes;
Tiny little bee
  Settles on his nose.

Great big dog
  Thinks it is a fly.
Never says a word,
  Winks very sly.

Tiny little bee,
  Tickles dog's nose —
Thinks like as not
  'Tis a pretty rose.

Dog smiles a smile,
  Winks his other eye,
Chuckles to himself
  How he'll catch a fly.

Then he makes a snap,
  Very quick and spry,
Does his level best,
  But doesn't catch the fly.

Tiny little bee,
  Alive and looking well;
Great big dog,
  Mostly gone to swell.

MORAL:

Dear friends and brothers all,
  Don't be too fast and free,
And when you catch a fly,
  Be sure it's not a bee.

GOBLIN MARKET

Morning and evening
Maids heard the goblins cry:
'Come buy our orchard fruits,
Come buy, come buy:
Apples and quinces,
Lemons and oranges,
Plump unpecked cherries,
Melons and raspberries,
Bloom-down-cheeked peaches,
Swart-headed mulberries,
Wild free-born cranberries,
Crab-apples, dewberries,
Pine-apples, blackberries,
Apricots, strawberries; —
All ripe together
In summer weather —
Morns that pass by,
Fair eves that fly;
Come buy, come buy;
Our grapes fresh from the vine,
Pomegranates full and fine,
Dates and sharp bullaces,
Rare peaches and greengages,
Damsons and bilberries,
Taste them and try:
Currants and gooseberries,
Bright fire-like barberries,
Figs to fill your mouth,
Citrons from the South,
Sweet to tongue and sound to eye;
Come buy, come buy.'

Christina Rossetti

National and Love of Country
Prayers, Graces and Thanksgivings
Lullabies and Cradle Songs

PART EIGHT

I vow to thee, my country – all earthly things above —
Entire and whole and perfect, the service of my love

LAND OF OUR BIRTH

Land of our Birth, we pledge to thee
Our love and toil in the years to be:
When we are grown and take our place,
As men and women with our race.

Father in Heaven who lovest all,
O help Thy children when they call,
That they may build from age to age
An undefilèd heritage.

Teach us to rule ourselves alway,
Controlled and cleanly night and day;
That we may bring, if need arise,
No maimed or worthless sacrifice.

Teach us the strength that cannot seek,
By deed or thought, to hurt the weak:
That, under Thee, we may possess
Man's Strength to comfort man's distress.

Teach us delight in simple things,
And Mirth that has no bitter springs;
Forgiveness free of evil done,
And Love to all men 'neath the sun!

Land of our Birth, our faith, our pride,
For whose dear sake our fathers died;
O Motherland, we pledge to thee
Head, heart and hand through the years to be.

Rudyard Kipling

THIS ENGLAND

This England never did, nor never shall,
Lie at the proud foot of a conqueror,
But when it first did help to wound itself.
Now these her princes are come home again,
Come the three corners of the world in arms,
And we shall shock them: naught shall make us rue,
If England to itself do rest but true.

Shakespeare

O ENGLAND, COUNTRY OF MY HEART'S DESIRE

O England, country of my heart's desire,
Land of the hedgerow and the village spire,
Land of thatched cottages and murmuring bees,
And wayside inns where one may take one's ease.
Of village green where cricket may be played
And fat old spaniels sleeping in the shade —
O homeland, far away across the main,
How would I love to see your face again! —
Your daisied meadows and your grassy hills,
Your primrose banks, your parks, your tinkling rills,
Your copses where the purple bluebells grow
Your quiet lanes where lovers loiter so,
Your cottage-gardens with their wallflower's scent,
Your swallows 'neath the eaves, your sweet content!
And 'mid the fleecy clouds that o'er you spread,
Listen, the skylark singing overhead —

    That's the old country, that's the old home!
    You never forget it wherever you roam.

E. Y. Lucas

I VOW TO THEE, MY COUNTRY

I vow to thee, my country – all earthly things above —
Entire and whole and perfect, the service of my love,
The love that asks no question: the love that stands the test,
That lays upon the altar the dearest and the best:
The love that never falters, the love that pays the price,
The love that makes undaunted the final sacrifice.

And there's another country, I've heard of long ago —
Most dear to them that love her, most great to them that know —
We may not count her armies; we may not see her King —
Her fortress is a faithful heart, her pride is suffering —
And soul by soul and silently her shining bounds increase,
And her ways are ways of gentleness and all her paths are Peace.

Sir Cecil Spring-Rice

THE TOY BAND

Dreary lay the long road, dreary lay the town,
   Lights out and never a glint o' moon:
Weary lay the stragglers, half a thousand down,
   Sad sighed the weary big Dragoon.
'Oh! if I'd a drum here to make them take the road again,
   Oh! if I'd a fife to wheedle – come, boys, come!
You that mean to fight it out, wake and take your load again,
   Fall in! Fall in! Follow the fife and drum!

'Hey, but here's a toy shop, here's a drum for me,
   Penny whistles too to play the tune!
Half a thousand dead men soon shall hear and see
   We're a band!' said the weary big Dragoon.
'Rubadub! Rubadub! Wake and take the road again,
   Wheedle-deedle-deedle-dee, come, boys, come!
You that mean to fight it out, wake and take your load again,
   Fall in! Fall in! Follow the fife and drum!'

Cheerly goes the dark road, cheerly goes the night,
   Cheerly goes the blood to keep the beat:
Half a thousand dead men marching on to fight
   With a little penny drum to lift their feet.
'Rubadub! Rubadub! Wake and take the road again,
   Wheedle-deedle-deedle-dee, come, boys, come!
You that mean to fight it out, wake and take your load again,
   Fall in! Fall in! Follow the fife and drum!'

As long as there's an Englishman to ask a tale of me,
   As long as I can tell the tale aright,
We'll not forget the penny whistle's wheedle-deedle-dee
   And the big Dragoon a-beating down the night,
'Rubadub! Rubadub! Wake and take the road again,
   Wheedle-deedle-deedle-dee, come, boys, come!
You that mean to fight it out, wake and take your load again
   Fall in! Fall in! Follow the fife and drum!'

Sir Henry Newbolt

JERUSALEM

And did those feet in ancient time
   Walk upon England's mountains green?
And was the holy Lamb of God
   On England's pleasant pastures seen?

And did the countenance divine
   Shine forth upon our clouded hills?
And was Jerusalem builded here
   Among these dark Satanic mills?

Bring me my bow of burning gold,
   Bring me my arrows of desire,
Bring me my spear, O clouds, unfold!
   Bring me my chariot of fire!

I will not cease from mental fight,
   Nor shall my sword sleep in my hand,
Till we have built Jerusalem
   In England's green and pleasant land.

William Blake

EVENING

Hush, hush, little baby,
   The sun's in the west;
The lamb in the meadow
   Has laid down to rest.

The bough rocks the bird now,
   The flower rocks the bee,
The wave rocks the lily,
   The wind rocks the tree;

And I rock the baby
   So softly to sleep —
It must not awaken
   Till daisy-buds peep.

THE UNION JACK

This little flag to us so dear,
   The Union Jack of Fame,
Come, sit by me, and you shall hear
   The way it got its name.

We first must look at other three,
   Please hold them up quite tight,
They all have crosses, you can see,
   Two red ones and one white.

St Patrick's Cross, to Ireland dear,
   Like letter X it lies;
St George's Cross, so bright and clear,
   Led England's battle cries.

St Andrew's Cross is white, you see,
   Upon a bed of blue,
The Scottish flag it used to be,
   To it the folks were true.

In course of time, the three combin'd,
   It was a famous tack:
We'll do the same, and you will find,
   Great Britain's Union Jack.

Jeannie Kirby

GRACE AND THANKSGIVING

We thank Thee, Lord, for quiet upland lawns,
For misty loveliness of autumn dawns,
For gold and russet of the ripened fruit,
For yet another year's fulfilment, Lord,
     We thank Thee now.

For joy of glowing colour, flash of wings,
We thank Thee, Lord; for all the little things
That make the love and laughter of our days,
For home and happiness and friends, we praise
     And thank Thee now.

Elizabeth Gould

A CHILD'S PRAYER

For Morn, my dome of blue,
  For Meadows green and gay,
And Buds who love the twilight of the leaves,
  Let Jesus keep me joyful when I pray.

For the big Bees that hum
  And hide in bells of flowers;
For the winding roads that come
  To Evening's holy door
May Jesus bring me grateful to His arms,
  And guard my innocence for evermore.

Siegfried Sassoon

EVENING SONG

Soft falls the night,
The day grows dim,
To Thee I lift my evening hymn,
O Lord of dark and light.

My hands I raise,
A little spire,
And send my voice up high and higher
To Thee in happy praise.

For home and friend,
For books and toys,
For all the countless loves and joys
That Thou dost daily send.

Close Thou mine eyes,
That when the day
Returns once more from far away,
I may rejoicing rise.

Edith King

A CHILD'S PRAYER

Father, we thank Thee for the night
And for the pleasant morning light,
For rest and food and loving care,
And all that makes the world so fair.
Help us to do the thing we should.
To be to others kind and good,
In all we do, in all we say,
To grow more loving every day.

MORNING THANKSGIVING

Thank God for sleep in the long quiet night,
   For the clear day calling through the little leaded panes,
For the shining well-water and the warm golden light,
   And the paths washed white by singing rains.

For the treasure of the garden, the gilly-flowers of gold,
   The prouder petalled tulips, the primrose full of spring,
For the crowded orchard boughs, and the swelling buds that hold
   A yet unwoven wonder, to Thee our praise we bring.

Thank God for good bread, for the honey in the comb,
   For the brown-shelled eggs, for the clustered blossom set
Beyond the open window in a pink and cloudy foam,
   For the laughing loves among the branches set.

For earth's little secret and innumerable ways,
   For the carol and the colour, Lord, we bring
What things may be of thanks, and that Thou has lent our days
   Eyes to see and ears to hear and lips to sing.

John Drinkwater

THE ROBIN'S SONG

God bless the field and bless the furrow
Stream and branch and rabbit burrow
Hill and stone and flower and tree,
From Britsil town to Wetherby —
Bless the sun and bless the sleet,
Bless the lane and bless the street,
Bless the night and bless the day,
From Somerset and all the way
To the meadows of Cathay;
Bless the minnow, bless the whale,
Bless the rainbow and the hail,
Bless the nest and bless the leaf,
Bless the righteous and the thief,
Bless the wing and bless the fin,
Bless the air I travel in,
Bless the mill and bless the mouse,
Bless the miller's bricken house,
Bless the earth and bless the sea,
God bless you and God bless me!

Old English Rhyme

HE PRAYETH WELL

He prayeth well, who loveth well
Both man and bird and beast,
He prayeth best, who loveth best
All things both great and small;
For the dear God who loveth us,
He made and loveth all.

Samuel Taylor Coleridge

GOOD NIGHT

Good night! Good night!
Far flies the light;
But still God's love
Shall shine above,
Making all bright,
Good night! Good night!

Victor Hugo

NOD

Softly along the road of evening,
   In a twilight dim with rose,
Wrinkled with age, and drenched with dew,
   Old Nod, the shepherd goes.

His drowsy flocks stream on before him.
   Their fleeces charged with gold,
To where the sun's last beam leans low
   On Nod the shepherd's fold.

The hedge is quick and green with briar,
   From their sand the conies creep;
And all the birds that fly in heaven
   Flock singing home to sleep.

His lambs outnumber a noon's roses,
   Yet, when night's shadows fall,
His blind old sheep-dog, Slumber-soon,
   Misses not one of all.

His are the quiet steeps of dreamland,
   The waters of no-more-pain,
His ram's bell rings 'neath an arch of stars,
   'Rest, rest, and rest again.'

Walter de la Mare

CRADLE HYMN

Away in a manger, no crib for a bed,
The little Lord Jesus laid down His sweet head.
The stars in the bright sky looked down where He lay —
The little Lord Jesus asleep in the hay.

The cattle are lowing, the Baby awakes,
But little Lord Jesus, no crying He makes.
I love Thee, Lord Jesus! look down from the sky,
And stay by my cradle till morning is nigh.

Martin Luther

CRADLE SONG

What does little birdie say
In her nest at peep of day?
Let me fly, says little birdie,
Mother, let me fly away.

Birdie, rest a little longer,
Till the little wings are stronger,
So she rests a little longer,
Then she flies away.

What does little baby say,
In her bed at peep of day?
Baby says, like little birdie,
Let me rise and fly away.

Baby, sleep a little longer,
Till the little limbs are stronger,
If she sleeps a little longer,
Baby too shall fly away.

Lord Tennyson

SWEET AND LOW

Sweet and low, sweet and low,
   Wind of the western sea,
Low, low, breathe and blow,
   Wind of the western sea!
Over the rolling waters go,
Come from the dropping moon and blow,
    Blow him again to me,
While my little one, while my pretty one sleeps.

Sleep and rest, sleep and rest,
Father will come to thee soon;
Rest, rest, on mother's breast,
Father will come to thee soon;
Father will come to his babe in the nest,
Silver sails all out of the west
Under the silver moon:
Sleep, my little one, sleep, my pretty one, sleep.

Lord Tennyson

THE UNWRITTEN SONG

Now where's a song for our small dear,
With her quaint voice and her quick ear,
To sing – for gnats and bats to hear —
    At twilight in her bed?
A song of tiny elfin things
With shiny, silky, silvery wings,
Footing it in fairy rings,
    And kissing overhead.

A song of starry glow-worms' lights
In the long grass of shadowy nights,
And flitting showers of firefly flights,
    Where summer woods hang deep;
Of hovering noiseless owls that find
Their way at dark; and of a kind
And drowsy, drowsy ocean wind
    That puts the sea to sleep.

But where's the song for our small dear,
With her quaint voice and her quick ear,
To sing – for dreamland things to hear —
    And hush herself to sleep?

Ford Madox Ford

Christmas and Easter Poems

PART NINE

Why do the bells of Christmas ring?
Why do little children sing?

THE OXEN

Christmas Eve, and twelve of the clock.
  'Now they are all on their knees,'
An elder said as we sat in a flock
  By the embers in fireside ease.

We pictured the meek mild creatures where
  They dwelt in their strawy pen,
Nor did it occur to one of us there
  To doubt they were kneeling then.

So fair a fancy few would weave
  In these years! Yet, I feel,
If someone said on Christmas Eve.
  'Come; see the oxen kneel.

'In the lonely barton by yonder coomb
  Our childhood used to know,'
I should go with him in the gloom,
  Hoping it might be so.

Thomas Hardy

A CHILD'S CHRISTMAS CAROL

There was a little Baby once
  Born upon Christmas Day;
The oxen lowed His lullabye
  As in His crib He lay:
His tree, it was a lonely tree
  That stood upon a hill,
Its candles were the mighty stars
  That shine upon us still;
His toys were flocks or little lambs,
  He loved to see them play:
It is for Him we are so glad,
  Now upon Christmas Day.

Christine Chaundler

THE CAROL SINGERS

Last night the carol singers came
    When I had gone to bed,
Upon the crisp white path outside
    I heard them softly tread.

I sat upright to listen, for
    I knew they came to tell,
Of all the things that happened on
    The very first Noel.

Upon my ceiling flickering
    I saw their lantern glow,
And then they sang their carols sweet
    Of Christmas long ago.

And when at last they went away,
    Their carol-singing done,
There was a little boy who wished
    They'd only just begun.

Margaret G. Rhodes

CRADLE SONG AT BETHLEHEM

Oh! hush Thee, oh! hush Thee, my Baby so small,
The ass hath her crib and the ox hath his stall,
They shelter Thee, Baby, from Heaven above,
Oh! hush Thee, oh! hush Thee, my Baby, my love.

Oh! hush Thee, oh! hush Thee, my Baby so small,
Dim is the light from the lamp on the wall,
Bright in the night sky shineth a star,
Leading the Kings who come from afar.

Oh! hush Thee, oh! hush Thee, my Baby so small,
Joseph is spreading the straw in the stall,
Soon wilt Thou sleep in the nook of my arm
Safe from all trouble and danger and harm.

E. J. Falconer

A CHRISTMAS CAROL

The Christ-child lay on Mary's lap,
  His hair was like a light.
(O weary, weary were the world,
  But here is all alright.)

The Christ-child lay on Mary's breast,
  His hair was like a star.
(O stern and cunning are the kings,
  But here the true hearts are.)

The Christ-child lay on Mary's heart,
  His hair was like a fire.
(O weary, weary is the world,
  But here the world's desire.)

The Christ-child stood at Mary's knee.
  His hair was like a crown,
And all the flowers looked up at Him,
  And all the stars looked down.

G. K. Chesterton

CHRISTMAS EVE

On Christmas Eve my mother read
  The story once again,
Of how the little Child was born,
  And of the Three Wise Men.

And how by following the Star
  They found Him where He lay,
And brought Him gifts; and that is why
  We keep our Christmas Day.

And when she read it all, I went
  And looked across the snow,
And thought of Jesus coming
  As He did so long ago.

I looked into the East, and saw
  A great star blazing bright;
There were three men upon the road
  All black against the light.

I thought I heard the angels sing,
  Away upon the hill . . .
I held my breath . . . it seemed as if
  The whole great world were still.

It seemed to me the little Child
  Was being born again . . .
And very near . . . and Then somehow
  Was Now . . . or Now was Then!

Edna Kingsley Wallace

THE CHRISTMAS PARTY

We're going to have a party
  And a lovely Christmas tea,
And flags and lighted candles
  Upon the Christmas Tree!

And silver balls and lanterns,
  Tied on with golden string,
Will hide among the branches
  By little bells that ring.

And then there will be crackers
  And caps and hats and toys,
A Christmas cake and presents
  For all the girls and boys.

With dancing, games and laughter,
  With music, songs and fun,
We'll make our Christmas Party
  A joy for everyone!

Adeline White

SANTA CLAUS

He comes in the night! He comes in the night!
 He softly, silently comes;
While the little brown heads on the pillows so white
 Are dreaming of bugles and drums.
He cuts through the snow like a ship through the foam,
 While the white flakes around him whirl;
Who tells him I know not, but he findeth the home
 Of each good little boy and girl.

His sleigh it is long, and deep, and wide;
 It will carry a host of things
While dozens of drums hang over the side,
 With the sticks sticking under the strings.
And yet not the sound of a drum is heard,
 Not a bugle blast is blown,
As he mounts to the chimney-top like a bird,
 And drops to the hearth like a stone.

The little red stockings he silently fills,
 Till the stockings will hold no more;
The bright little sleds for the great snow hills
 Are quickly set down on the floor.
Then Santa Claus mounts to the roof like a bird,
 And glides to his seat in the sleigh;
Not the sound of a bugle or drum is heard
 As he noiselessly gallops away.

He rides to the East, and he rides to the West,
 Of his goodies he touches not one;
He eateth the crumbs of the Christmas feast
 When the dear little folks are done.
Old Santa Claus doeth all that he can;
 This beautiful mission is his;
Then, children, be good to the little old man,
 When you find who the little man is.

A CHRISTMAS SONG

Winds through the Olive trees softly did blow
Round little Bethlehem long, long ago.
Sheep on the hill-sides lay white as the snow;
Shepherds were watching them long, long ago,
Shepherds were watching them long, long ago.

Then from the happy skies Angels bent low,
Singing their songs of joy, long, long ago.
For, in His manger bed, cradles, we know,
Christ came to Bethlehem long, long ago,
Christ came to Bethlehem long, long ago.

PUDDING CHARMS

Our Christmas pudding was made in November,
All they put in it, I quite well remember:
Currants and raisins, and sugar and spice,
Orange peel, lemon peel – everything nice
Mixed up together, and put in a pan.
'When you've stirred it,' said Mother, 'as much as you can,
We'll cover it over, that nothing may spoil it,
And then, in the copper, tomorrow we'll boil it.'
That night, when we children were all fast asleep,
A real fairy godmother came crip-a-creep!

She wore a red cloak, and a tall steeple hat
(Though nobody saw her but Tinker, the cat!)
And out of her pocket a thimble she drew,
A button of silver, a silver horse-shoe,
And, whisp'ring a charm, in the pudding pan popped them,
Then flew up the chimney directly she dropped them;
And even old Tinker pretended he slept
(With Tinker a secret is sure to be kept!),
So nobody knew, until Christmas came round,
And there, in the pudding, these treasures we found.

Charlotte Druitt Cole

SONG

Why do the bells of Christmas ring?
Why do little children sing?

Once a lovely shining star,
Seen by shepherds from afar,
Gently moved until its light
Made a manger's cradle bright.

There a darling baby lay,
Pillowed soft upon the hay.
And its Mother sung and smiled:
'This is Christ, the holy Child!'

Therefore bells for Christmas ring,
Therefore little children sing.

Eugene Field

THE NEW YEAR

I am the little New Year, ho, ho!
Here I come tripping it over the snow.
Shaking my bells with a merry din —
So open your doors and let me in!

Presents I bring for each and all —
Big folks, little folks, short and tall;
Each one from me a treasure may win —
So open your doors and let me in!

Some shall have silver and some shall have gold,
Some shall have new clothes and some shall have old;
Some shall have brass and some shall have tin —
So open your doors and let me in!

Some shall have water and some shall have milk,
Some shall have satin and some shall have silk!
But each from me a present may win —
So open your doors and let me in!

'HOW FAR IS IT TO BETHLEHEM?'

How far is it to Bethlehem?
 Not very far.
Shall we find the stable-room
 Lit by a star?

Can we see the little Child?
 Is He within?
If we lift the wooden latch,
 May we go in?

May we stroke the creatures there —
 Ox, ass, or sheep?
May we peep like them and see
 Jesus asleep?

If we touch His tiny hand,
 Will He awake?
Will He know we've come so far
 Just for His sake?

Great kings have precious gifts,
 And we have naught;
Little smiles and little tears
 Are all we brought.

For all weary children
 Mary must weep;
Here, on His bed of straw,
 Sleep, children, sleep.

God, in His mother's arms,
 Babes in the byre,
Sleep, as they sleep who find
 Their heart's desire.

Frances Chesterton

EASTER

I got me flowers to straw Thy way,
I got me boughs off many a tree;
But Thou wast up by break of day,
And brought'st Thy sweets along with Thee.

Yet though my flowers be lost, they say
A heart can never come too late;
Teach it to sing Thy praise this day,
And then this day my life shall date.

George Herbert

WHEN MARY THRO' THE GARDEN WENT

When Mary thro' the garden went,
There was no sound of any bird,
And yet, because the night was spent,
The little grasses lightly stirred,
The flowers awoke, the lilies heard.

When Mary thro' the garden went,
The dew lay still on flower and grass,
The waving palms above her sent
Their fragrance out as she did pass,
No light upon the branches was.

When Mary thro' the garden went,
Her eyes, for weeping long, were dim.
The grass beneath her footsteps bent,
The solemn lilies, white and slim,
These also stood and wept for Him.

When Mary thro' the garden went,
She sought, within the garden ground,
One for whom her heart was rent,
One who for her sake was bound,
One who sought and she was found.

Mary E. Coleridge

ENVOI

Earth puts her colours by,
And veils her in one whispering cloak of shadow;
Green goes from the meadow,
Red leaves and flowers and shining pools are shrouded;
A few stars sail upon a windy sky,
And the moon is clouded.

The delicate music, traced
In and out of the soft lights and the laughter,
Is hushed, round ledge and rafter
The last faint echoes into silence creeping;
The harp is mute, the violins encased,
And the singers sleeping:

So, now my songs are done,
Leave me tonight awhile and the starlight gleaming,
To silence and sweet dreaming,
Here where no music calls, no beauty shakes me;
Till in my heart the birds sing to the sun
And the new dawn wakes me.

P. H. B. Lyon

233

INDEX OF TITLES

INDEX OF TITLES

INDEX OF TITLES

INDEX OF TITLES

INDEX OF FIRST LINES

INDEX OF FIRST LINES

INDEX OF FIRST LINES

INDEX OF FIRST LINES

INDEX OF FIRST LINES

INDEX OF AUTHORS

INDEX OF AUTHORS

INDEX OF AUTHORS

INDEX OF AUTHORS

INDEX OF AUTHORS

INDEX OF AUTHORS

ACKNOWLEDGMENTS

For permission to use copyright material we are indebted to the following authors, literary executors and publishers:

Miss O. Ault for 'The Pig's Tail' from *Dreamland Shores* by Norman Ault; Miss Jean Ayer and The Macmillan Company of New York for 'Everyday Things'; Miss Enid Blyton for 'What Piggy-Wig Found' and 'Winter', and Messrs Methuen and Miss Blyton for 'The Field Mouse'; Mrs Bennett for 'Little Brown Seed', 'Mrs Jenny Wren' and 'Robin's Song' by Rodney Bennett; Messrs A. & C. Black for 'Five Little Brothers' by Ella Wheeler Wilcox; Messrs Blackie & Sons Ltd for 'The Frog and the Bird' by Vera Hessey, 'The Old Brown Horse' by W. K.

Holmes, 'Strange Talk' by L. E. Yates, 'Trains' by Hope Shepherd, 'The Silver Road' by Hamish Hendry and 'Three Dogs' by E. C. Brereton; Messrs Basil Blackwell & Mott Ltd, and the authors for 'Evening Song', 'Cobwebs', 'Pebbles', 'The Rabbit' and 'To the Bat' by Edith King, and 'The Lighthouse and 'Through the Porthole' by Marjorie Wilson. Miss Joyce Brisley for 'The Two Families'. Messrs Jonathan Cape and the Mary Webb Estate for 'Foxgloves' and 'Secret Joy' from *Poems and the Spring of Joy* by Mary Webb, 'Goldenhair' by James Joyce and Mrs W. H. Davies for 'Leisure' and 'The Rain' by W. H. Davies. Miss Christine Chaundler and Messrs Christie & Moore Ltd for 'The Tree in the Garden' and 'A Child's Christmas Carol' from *The Golden Years* (Robert Hale); Mrs Chesterman for 'A Rhyme Sheet of Other Lands' by Hugh Chesterman; The Clarendon Press, Oxford, for 'The Cliff-top' and 'Gay Robin Is Seen No More' from *The Shorter Poems of Robert Bridges*. Mr Edmund Eyre for 'The Journey' from *Songs and Poems of Richmond Hill* by Aidan Clarke. Messrs Wm. Collins, Sons & Co. Ltd and the authors for 'The Clothes Line' by Charlotte Druitt Cole, 'The Carol Singers' by Margaret Rhodes, 'Water' by John R. Crossland and the following poems from *Underneath a Mushroom* (Laurel and Gold Series), 'Sun and Moon' by Charlotte Druitt Cole, 'The Little Men' by Flora Fearne and 'The Kite' and 'My Little Dog' by Pearl Forbes MacEwan; Mr Padraic Colum for 'The Old Woman of the Roads'; Messrs Constable & Co. Ltd and the author for 'Envoi' by P. H. B. Lyon. Messrs J. M. Dent & Sons Ltd and the author for 'The Witch' by Percy Ilott; Messrs Gerald Duckworth & Co Ltd for 'The Elephant' by Hilaire Belloc. Messrs E. A. Dutton & Co. Inc. for 'Christmas Eve' from *Feelings and Things* by Edna Kingsley Wallace; Miss Eleanor Farjeon for 'The Flower Seller', 'The Night Will Never Stay' and 'There are Big Waves'; Miss Elizabeth Fleming for 'The Hedgehog and His Coat', 'In the Mirror', 'Toadstools' and 'The Window Cleaner'; Mr Michael A. E. Franklin for 'The Scarecrow'. Miss Elizabeth Gould for 'Midsummer Night'; Miss Marjorie Greenfield for 'Things I Like'; Messrs George G. Harrap & Co. Ltd and the authors for 'The Kind Mousie' by Natalie Joan, 'The Bird Bath' and 'Who?' by Florence Hoatson, 'What the Thrush Says' by Queenie Scott-Hopper and 'April' from *Poems of Sir William Watson, 1878–1935*. Messrs William Heinemann Ltd for 'Prayers for Gentleness

ACKNOWLEDGMENTS

to all Creatures' from *Collected Poems* by John Galsworthy; Messrs John Lane The Bodley Head Ltd and the author for 'Child's Song in Spring' by E. Nesbitt from *A Pomander of Verse*. The Little Gem Poetry Books, Bk. I (G. Bell & Sons Ltd) for 'A Christmas Song'; Messrs Longmans, Green & Co. Ltd and Lady Spring-Rice for 'Day' and 'I Vow to Thee My Country' from *Poems* by Sir Cecil Spring-Rice. Messrs Macmillan & Co. Ltd for 'A Frolic' from *Collected Poems by A. E.*, 'The Oxen' by Thomas Hardy (by permission of the Trustees of the Hardy Estate), 'The Children's Song' from *Puck of Pook's Hill* by Rudyard Kipling (also by permission of Mrs Bambridge and of the Macmillan Co. of Canada), and Mrs Stephens for 'Danny Murphy', 'The Fifteen Acres', 'The Rivals', 'White Fields' and 'The Wood of Flowers' from *Collected Poems* by James Stephens. Mr Walter de la Mare and Messrs Faber & Faber Ltd for 'Nicholas Nye', 'Nod', 'Silver' and 'Sooeep!'; Messrs Methuen & Co. Ltd for 'Duck's Ditty' by Kenneth Grahame, 'Johnny's Farm' by H. M. Adams, 'Michael Met a White Duck' by J. Dupuy, and 'Puppy and I' by A. A. Milne; Mrs Alida Monro for 'Milk for the Cat' and 'One Blackbird' by Harold Monro. Messrs A. D. Peters for 'The Idlers' by Edmund Blunden and 'The Early Morning' by Hilaire Belloc; *The Poetry Review* for 'Apple Blossoms' by Helen Adams Parker; The Proprietors of *Punch* for 'The Watchmaker's Shop' by Elizabeth Fleming. Miss Dorothy Una Ratcliffe for 'The Pirates' Tea Party' from *Rosemary Isle* (Thomas Nelson & Sons Ltd); Mr Clive Sansom and Messrs A. C. Black Ltd for 'The Dustman', 'The Milkman' and 'The Postman' from *Speech Rhymes*; Mr Siegfried Sassoon and Messrs Faber & Faber Ltd for 'A Child's Prayer'; Messrs J. Saville & Co. Ltd for 'Fairy Music' by Enid Blyton; Messrs Sidgwick & Jackson Ltd and the author's representatives for 'The Elephant' by Herbert Asquith from *Poems 1912–1933*, 'Child's Song' from *Poems* by Gerald Gould, 'Four and Eight' from *Collected Poems* by ffrida Wolfe, and 'Moonlit Apples' and 'Morning Thanksgiving' from *The Very Thing* by John Drinkwater; Dame Edith Sitwell and Messrs Pearn, Pollinger & Higham Ltd for 'The King of China's Daughter'. The Society of Authors and the authors for 'Whale' by Geoffrey Dearmer, 'Conversation', 'The Donkey', 'The Fairy Flute', 'The Goblin', 'Mice' and 'Mrs Brown' by Rose Fyleman, 'Roadways' and 'Tewkesbury Road' from *Collected Poems* by John Masefield (also by

ACKNOWLEDGMENTS

permission of The Macmillan Company of Canada), to Mrs Binyon for 'The Little Dancers' by Laurence Binyon, and to Miss Pamela Hinkson for 'Pink Almond' and 'The Nightingale' by Katharine Tynan. Mr Wilfrid Thorley for 'Fan the Filly' and 'Song for a Ball Game'. The University of London Press Ltd for 'Harvest Song' and 'Shell Secrets' from *The London Treasury of Nursery Rhymes* (ed. J. Murray McBain). Messrs A. P. Watt & Son and the authors or executors for 'Jack o' the Inkpot' from *The Education of Uncle Paul* by Algernon Blackwood, 'How Far is it to Bethlehem?' by Frances Chesterton, 'A Christmas Carol' by G. K. Chesterton from *The White Knight* (J. M. Dent & Sons), 'The Train' and 'When Mary thro' the Garden Went' from *The Collected Poems of Mary E. Coleridge* (Rupert Hart-Davis), 'I'd love to be a Fairy's Child' by Robert Graves, 'The Barrel Organ', 'The New Duckling' and 'Sherwood' from *Collected Poems of Alfred Noyes* (also by permission of Messrs Wm. Blackwood & Sons), and 'The Toy Band' by Sir Henry Newbolt from *Poems Old and New* (John Murray Ltd); Messrs Frederick Warne & Co Ltd for 'The Owl and the Pussy Cat' from *Nonsense Songs* by Edward Lear; Messrs Williams & Norgate Ltd for 'Wandering Jack' by Émile Jacot from *Nursery Verseries*; Messrs Wells, Gardner & Darton Ltd for 'O England, Country of My Heart's Desire' and 'The Windmill' by E. V. Lucas, and 'Snow in Town' by Rickman Mark; and T. Werner Laurie Ltd for 'Songs' by Eugene Field.

Every effort has been made to trace the owners of copyrights, but we take this oportunity of tendering apologies to any owners whose rights may have been unwittingly infringed.